D1191511

DECK-STERITY

By

HARRY LORAYNE

Author of

CLOSE-UP CARD MAGIC

PERSONAL SECRETS

MY FAVORITE CARD TRICKS

HOW TO DEVELOP A SUPER-POWER MEMORY

SECRETS OF MIND POWER

INSTANT MIND POWER

MIRACLE MATH

ETC.

FIRST EDITION

Cover Design by **ED MISHELL**
Illustrated by **WILLIAM A. MORALES**

Contents

		Page
Forward		5
The 'Kick' Double-Lift		8
Double-Lift Gag		11
Double Put-Down		13
Double Trouble		14
Caught!		15
Spellbinder		16
Flip-Over Locator		20
Foursome		23
The Magic Step		30
New-Fangled Color Change		35
Outrageous Revelation		40
Outrageous Revelation #2		42
That Burns Me Up!		43
The Card Pyramid		45
Out Of This World Memory		55
Double Billemma		58
The Indicator		62
Oh, Those Aces!		69
Ten Card Poker Deal		72
Cointrol		83
The Royal Lovers		86
Faro Blockbuster		92
One-Eyed Jack Sandwich Sequel		100
Modernized Slop Shuffle		103
Mental Photography		105
1-2-3 Aces		111
About Faces		117
Favorite Aces & Kings		122
Stabbed in the Pack		129
Strip-Out Sleight		133
Vice Triumphant		135
Trampoline		138
Flying Aces		140
The Choice Is Yours		144
To Change A Card		147
Deal and Duck		149
Last Word		154

HARRY LORAYNE

FOREWORD

I ALMOST selected the title, "Runnin' Wild" for this book because for some reason, it seemed to relay my feelings about card magic in this era of 'swingers, hippies, beatniks, mini skirts,' and the 'go-go' feeling, in general.

Although I doubt if any card trick will ever take attention away from a mini-skirted young lady doing the frug—I do believe it's necessary for card magic to be modernized. It must be *entertaining*, above all.

I've always felt that way and I like to believe that most of the magic in all my books has 'filled the bill.' The days of the 'deal three piles; subtract seven cards and add four cards; put the deck behind your back and count 37, turn face up, then count 29, etc.;' type of trick, are (and have been) gone for some time now. But, unfortunately, too many 'magicians' aren't aware of it yet.

The speed with which everything moves today seems to have drastically shortened attention spans. Unless your audience is particularly interested in magic, or it consists of other magicians, you'd better grasp that attention quickly, by offering something new and different—and most important, by *entertaining*.

Of course, I can't make an entertainer out of you. I *can* include effects and routines in my books with which I know *I* can interest and entertain most any kind of audience. They're effects which I feel have the interest and entertainment value 'built in.'

I can also write them up as clearly as I possibly can; including all the 'touches' and the patter and presentation I feel I can, without making a 'book' of each effect. It's up to you to take it from there.

Again, as in my other books, many of the card effects do not have a 'pick-a-card' opening. Nothing wrong with such an opening, of course, but as I've said before, it's nice *not* to begin a card effect that way every once in a while, just as a change of pace.

Basically, I think the effects and routines I've included in this book fit the picture I've painted pertaining to the era in which we live.

To my knowledge, all the routines and effects are of my own conception, except where otherwise mentioned. These are 'audience tested' and 'audience preferred' effects. I have *never* included an effect in any of my books that did *not* fit these categories. Mostly, they're things I've used for years; but even if it's a new idea, I always try it out on both magicians and laymen before including it in any book.

I mention, a few times, in the text, that certain effects are difficult to describe. This is not just idle chatter—they *were* difficult to describe. They were not included in my earlier books mainly for that reason.

I include them now for two reasons:—No one remains on a stationary intellectual plateau. We learn continuously. What I mean is, I think that every book I've written has been better and more clearly written than the preceding one.

I probably couldn't have explained effects like 'Foursome' and 'The Indicator' in my first books—not according to my own standards, anyway. I've learned quite a bit about writing as I've continued to write. I think (and I hope) that the effects are explained, described and taught in this book just as clearly and concisely as possible.

That's one reason. The other reason for including these effects is:—I think that those of you who buy, or read, my magic books have become accustomed to my style. I think that by now, you know what to expect, and—you like it and understand it, or you wouldn't buy the book! So—I must assume that you *will* be able to do the routines I teach.

I mention my other magic books every once in a while. I do this only to tell you of certain sleights that are described in detail in those books; and where you'd find them in the books. I didn't think it fair to repeat those detailed descriptions here.

I originally had no intention of including 'Ten Card Poker Deal' because the basic idea has appeared in print before—a few times. But my friend and publisher, Louis Tannen, insisted. So, for what it's worth, the exact routine I've used for years *is* included.

If you think Lou was right in insisting I include it, let him know; if you think he was wrong, do me a favor and forget about it, will you!?

'Seriously though, folks,' a lot of time and work goes into writing these routines in complete detail—please don't start changing them around until you've learned them *as* I teach them. After that, of course, it's up to you.

Also included in this book are some routines with objects other than cards. This is the first time I've done this. But they are close-up effects which I've used through the years, and I see no reason for not including them.

In my first magic book, *Close-Up Card Magic,* I included some moves and effects that I had previously contributed to magic magazines. I found that many magicians liked the idea. They had missed that particular issue of the magazine, perhaps—and even if they hadn't, the effect was, of course, brought up to date in the book. And, as magicians have told me, it saved them looking through hundreds of magazines in order to find a particular effect of mine.

I've done the same thing in this book, with three or four routines. I think the effects are worth reminding you of, if you did read them in the magazines originally; and if you didn't, I think they're worth your attention now. I hope you agree with me. (I'll make a confession. I also feel that many more people buy my books than buy the magazines—so more people will get to read these routines. It's *ego,* is what it is!)

And again, don't overlook the Afterthoughts. I sometimes come up with a good idea or two after I've written an effect and those ideas are in the Afterthoughts.

Well, have fun!

THE 'KICK' DOUBLE-LIFT

THERE are probably already hundreds of methods for doing the double-lift. I taught one or two of my own in my book, *Close-Up Card Magic*. But I guess there's always room for one more. I've been using this method quite often lately, and I find it to be sure fire, easy to do and pretty natural looking.

I don't expect it to shake the magical world—it still necessitates a get-ready, and there are easier ways to do a double-lift—but I think I should get it on record and let you decide whether you want to use it or not. Every magician I've shown it to, has reacted quite enthusiastically to it. (The same goes for 'Double Put-Down,' which is a derivation of this.)

So—hold the deck face down in your left hand. Hold it down on the palm, not up at the fingertips. The deck, of course, is well squared; the four fingers are at the right long side of the deck, and the left thumb is lying crossways on top.

The right hand approaches from above. Thumb rests at inner end, second, third and fourth fingers at outer end, and forefinger bent and resting on top.

The ball of the right thumb presses lightly and lifts one card slightly at inner end. It now bends in slightly and lifts another card. This is the thumb-count, of course, and it insures lifting only two cards. (See Fig. 1).

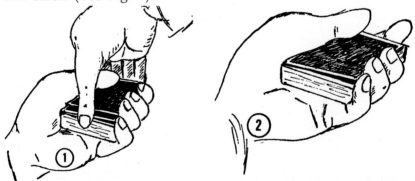

If the thumb tip bends in just a bit now, the upper card will fall and align with the second card. The left thumb pressing down on top of the deck insures that nothing changes or moves at the front end.

Now press the *left little fingertip* inward ever so slightly as you remove the right hand. The *flesh* of the little fingertip holds the break. Do *not* put the fingertip *into* the break. (See Fig. 2).

That's the get-ready. It takes no more than a split-second and is imperceptible. There should be a short pause here, before actually doing the lift.

This is a bit difficult to describe, but here goes: When you're ready to do the lift, you do two things simultaneously. The right hand approaches the deck—that's the easy part. The second (and more important) thing is the one that's not easy to describe. The left second, third and little fingers *close down* onto the deck as the left thumb moves out of the way. (See Fig. 3).

As you can see by the figure, this *automatically* tilts (or 'kicks') the top two cards only, and perfectly aligned, to the left—at the inner end of the deck. This is the basis of the move. If you try it once or twice, you'll see that it *does* work automatically. Just don't think about it as you do it. Simply do it and it will work. There's a certain 'knack' involved, which may take a few tries—give it the few tries and you'll see what I mean.

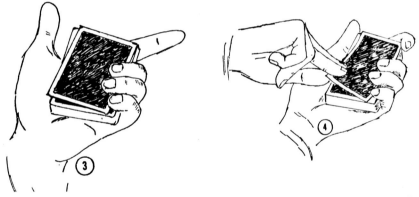

Okay; by this time the right hand is over the deck. The right thumb tip goes under the protruding corners, and the first and second fingertips above. (See Fig. 4). Turn the card(s) over (face up) toward the right, like the page of a book, placing it face up and injogged onto the deck. The left fingertips keep the cards aligned. (See Fig. 5). Actually, it isn't necessary for the thumb tip to go *under* this protruding corner immediately. Just pressing the thumb *against* the corners will do it. Try it once and see.

To turn the lift down, reverse the action. Grasp the card(s) at the inner left corner, turn like the page of a book, and leave it *injogged* on the deck. The last step is to push the card(s) flush with the right thumb tip. (See Fig. 6). The base of the left thumb and the left fingers act as runners, keeping the card(s) in perfect alignment.

Practice this in a four-step beat. Do the get-ready and then, Step 1: Close (or bend downward) the left fingertips so that the cards tilt at the inner end. Step 2: Turn the card(s) face up. Step 3: Turn the card(s) face down. Step 4: Push the card(s) flush with the right thumb tip.

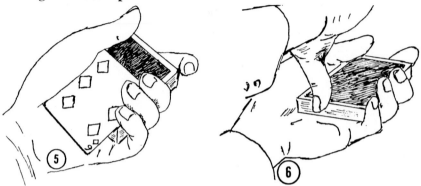

After some practice, when you're accustomed to this, you'll find that a three-step beat is all that's necessary. Steps one and two will blend into one.

Anyway, although I don't know if you'll agree with me, when you've practiced for just a short while, I think you may decide that this is as good a double-lift as any. That's up to you.

Afterthoughts:—There isn't much more I can tell you about this, except perhaps that after you learn to turn the card(s) face up as I've explained, you can turn them face down any way you like.

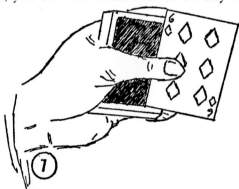

I do it as described most of the time. But you can, if you like, move the face up card(s) up onto the left fingertips, holding them with the thumb, as in (Fig. 7)—then flip the card(s) face down with the right fingers. The right fingers simply go under the right long side of the card(s)—and flip.

Or any way you like. I'd suggest you learn it as I've taught it, first.

The break held by the flesh of the left little fingertip can be as slight as you want it to be. The larger the break, the more you will expose the corner of the card(s) to be lifted. You'll find that just the slightest fraction is all that's necessary.

(My friend, Cliff Green, devoted one paragraph to a vaguely similar idea in his wonderful book, *Professional Card Magic*. You might want to check it to see the difference in thinking.)

DOUBLE-LIFT GAG

THE DOUBLE-LIFT I just described reminded me of a gag I've used for years. It doesn't mean much for other magicians, but it will fool laymen. It's another non-earth shaking thing, but you may be surprised at the reaction you'll get with it.

While shuffling the deck, do some talk pertaining to 'matter passing through matter.'

Do a double-lift, naming the exposed card (say it's the 4D). Turn it face down on the deck, and hold the deck face down and squared in the left hand. You can hold it either down on the palm or up near the fingertips. Try both ways and use the one that's better for you. Whichever you use, the left forefinger should be resting at the outer end of the deck.

Suiting action to words, say, "If I take this 4D and push it into the deck at this end . . ." Here you take the top card only and push it about an inch into the center of the deck, at the inner end. (See Fig 8).

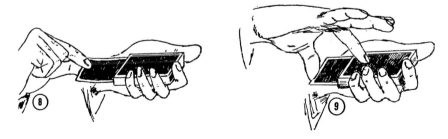

"And if I push it flush like this, you'll see that it travels right through the deck and out the other end."

Again, suiting action to words, place your right thumbtip on the inner end of the protruding card and rest your second fingertip on top of the deck, near the inner end. (See Fig. 9).

The right hand moves forward sharply—the thumb pushing the indifferent card flush and the second fingertip pushing the top card (4D) off the deck onto the table. It should fall *face down*. And— the indifferent card going into the deck and the 4D moving off the deck are simultaneous actions.

To facilitate the top card moving off the deck, do this: Start the move slowly to give you a chance to put your left forefinger tip *under* the top card, pushing it slightly upward. (See Fig. 10). This will, as I said, facilitate the action, helping the top card to leave the deck.

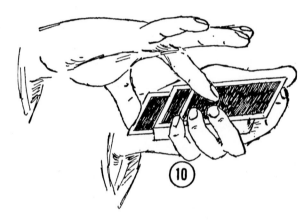

With a minimum of practice, you'll be able to shoot that top card six inches or so from the deck. The idea here is that it should appear as if you're seriously trying to make the spectator believe that the card is traveling through the center of the deck. So do it that way, although no matter what, it will be obvious that you're pushing it off the top.

I'm sure you know what I mean, although the thought is hard to get onto paper. Basically, it's a 'sucker gag.' Your last remark should be, "And there's the 4D, after traveling right through the deck." Point to the card on the table as you say this.

The reactions of your spectators will vary, but basically, I think you'll find that he'll look at you and say, "Oh, come on, that's not the 4D; that card came from the top"—or something to that effect.

That leads you to your ending. Turn up the tabled card (the 4D), saying, "I'm surprised at you. I wouldn't kid you for the world!"—and leave him completely confused.

Afterthoughts:—I think you'll have to try this on laymen a few times before you can appreciate it. It's a real quickie, so you can try it without wasting any time.

Your attitude during the performance is something you'll have to fit to your own personality. Done correctly, it's a good quickie 'sucker gag.'

DOUBLE PUT-DOWN

I DON'T want to devote too much space to this, but there are some effects where it is necessary to place two cards face up (or face down) on the table and make them look like one card.

This is easily accomplished using the little finger 'kick' I taught you in the 'Kick' Double-Lift. It's done with the left hand only, except for the get-ready.

Do the get-ready, forming a fairly wide break. Now do the 'kick' move *as* you turn the hand over, turning the deck face up. Keep the left fingers pressed tightly so that the two cards stay aligned. (See Fig. 11) The hand turns over as it moves toward the table top.

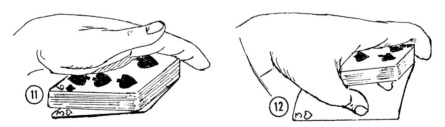

With a little practice, you'll be able to bend the thumb inward so that the tip can push down on the exposed corner(s). In actual practice, you may find that it's easier for the thumbtip to hit at the protruding *side* of the card(s), instead of the corner. (See Fig. 12).

Bend the thumb in so that it can press the card(s) lightly onto the table, *then* relax the other fingers and lift the hand and the deck straight up and away. The thumb tip is the *last* to leave the card(s). (See Fig. 13). This insures that the two cards stay in alignment.

Learn to do it without hesitation at the actual put-down, and it looks good. Although it may *feel* unnatural to you (at first), it *looks* natural enough. And—placing the card(s) under your spectator's nose, will help to conceal the double thickness. The move can be repeated rapidly two or three times, or as often as desired.

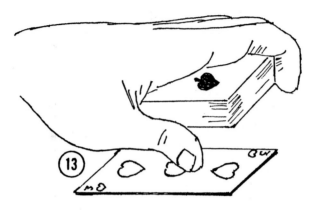

Although the following can be done with standard double-lifts, I thought I'd include them just to demonstrate how the Double Put-Down can be used. For the record, I'll call this

DOUBLE TROUBLE

The bare bones:—Have two cards selected and returned. Control them so that one card is on top and the other is *third* from the top. I'll leave this to you.

Do the Double Put-Down twice in a row, exposing two indifferent cards. The patter covering this is that you think you've found the two cards, etc., and here they are. Place the cards side by side.

When the spectators deny that these are their cards, cut the deck in half and place a half, face up, neatly onto each of the tabled cards.

Turn the halves face down. Pick up the top card of each half, one in each hand. Hold them face down and say, "These are not your cards? Well, what were your cards?"

When they answer, repeat the names, turn the two cards you're holding face up, simultaneously, and say, "That's what I said—these are your cards!"

CAUGHT!

Again, just the bare bones, to give you something to think about. Control (or force) a card. Look for your **two** 'detective' cards. If the selected card is red, use, say, the black sixes; if the selected card is black, use a red pair.

Let's assume that you're using the black sixes as the detective cards. Control it so that the selection and the sixes are on top, with the selection *between* the sixes. I'm leaving the controls, etc., to you. As I said, I'm including these to show you how the Double Put-Down can be used, not because I think they're particularly good effects; although they're not *bad*, either.

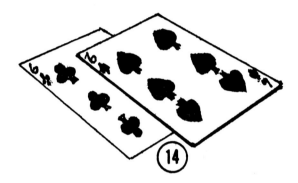

After some shuffling and patter about your detective cards, do the *exact* actions as you would for the Double Put-Down, but put down only *one* card; a black six. (Break only one card and actually do the move.)

Now, do the Double Put-Down, exposing the other black six. Put it down overlapping the first six. This is quite deceptive. (See Fig. 14).

Place the deck *face down* onto the two(?) black, face up, sixes. Square and cut the deck. Riffle the ends or snap your fingers, etc., and spread the deck in your hands, face up, exposing *three* face down cards in the center. Turn an end card face up and replace it, showing a black six. Turn up and replace the other end card, exposing the other black six.

You're holding a spread deck now, with a face down card between two black sixes. The patter is that the detectives have caught a card. Ask for the name of the selected card, and turn up the face down card, to end.

Afterthoughts:—Practice the Double Put-Down; you'll find it to be quite practical. Incidentally, I usually am standing when I do the move.

The two effects I've included are all right (I like 'Caught!' better), but to repeat, I mainly wanted to show you one or two ways of using the Put-Down.

It comes in handy if you need a method of secretly adding one card to a count. You'd do the Double Put-Down on the count of 'one,' then deal and count cards onto that in the same manner. Deal the second and third cards carefully and in such a way as to cover the first card(s). This is to hide any spreading of the two cards.

And—there's another use for the 'kick' move which I describe in "1-2-3 Aces," in this book.

Frankly, all I had in mind when I started this section was to teach you my little finger 'kick' method of the double-lift. I just did a bit of brainstorming once I started. I hope you've found it interesting, and perhaps learned something!

SPELLBINDER

A LTHOUGH I have come up with some spelling ideas (see "Favorite Aces and Kings"), I'm not particularly addicted to effects which terminate by simply spelling a spectator's card. I also prefer not to use crimped cards as a modus operandi if I can avoid it.

So—here's an effect which I terminate by simply spelling a spectator's card, and crimped cards help me do it!

I use this because when I do end an effect by spelling a spectator's card, I want it to appear as if there is no conceivable way of my knowing what or where the card is—and—I want to end by placing the deck on the table and making a big to-do about the fact that I'll spell the card from the top, a letter per card, without changing a card. I make this statement before I ask for the name of the card. Now, it becomes a strong effect, to my mind.

The basis of the effect is that any card can be spelled to, if it is set at twelfth from the top. For a few cards, the word 'of' is omitted, and sometimes the last letter 's' of the suit of a card is omitted. Keeping this in mind, all cards (but eight) can be spelled with 11 or 12 letters.

The eight exceptions are the ace, 2, 6 and 10 of clubs, and the 3, 7, 8 and queen of diamonds. For these club cards, you'd have to spell out the word 'the' and omit the last letter 's' in order to reach

12 letters. And, for these diamond cards, you'd have to omit the 'of' *and* the last 's' in order to spell each one with 12 letters.

If you don't mind spelling the 2C as, "Deuce of Clubs," then that is no longer an exception, because now it spells with exactly 12 letters. So we're left with only seven exceptions.

Now then, I personally don't care if one of these seven cards is selected, because I can make the spelling seem legitimate and as if that is the way I would have spelled *any* card. But I'll show you how to eliminate these seven cards as selections, if you like.

So finally—here's the effect, method and presentation:—If you don't care about eliminating the seven cards we spoke about, crimp the top (or bottom) five cards downward lengthwise. If you want to eliminate the exceptions: during a previous trick, get any five of the exceptions to the top (or bottom) and crimp *them*. (If you're afraid to take the chance of leaving even two of the exceptions available, get all seven to the top, but crimp only five.)

Shuffle the deck, retaining the five crimped cards on top. Then fairly shuffle about half the deck onto them, bringing the crimped cards to about center. (See Fig. 15). The size of the crimp in the figure is enlarged, of course, just to show you direction and position.

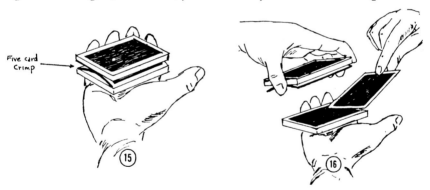

Five card Crimp →

⑮　⑯

Now spread the deck between your hands and have a card selected. Just be sure that one of the crimped cards is *not* taken. (If you've placed the 6th and 7th exceptions under the crimped cards; don't allow them to be selected either.)

If you like, you can do a table ribbon spread for the selection. Just try not to spread the center portion, so that the spectator can't take one of the crimped cards. I leave this to you. The important thing is to make sure the spectator *knows* that he has a completely free choice. (It certainly shouldn't be difficult for you to do this when you have to force one of 47 (or 45) cards!)

He remembers his card as you square the deck. Now cut at the *ends* of the deck for the replacement. (See Fig. 16) The crimp enables you to cut so that the selected card is replaced in the center of the deck directly *beneath* the five crimped cards. (This is done without looking or hesitating.)

Obviously square the deck, proving that the card is lost. Now do a one-hand Charlier cut, which will automatically bring the crimped cards (with the selection beneath them) to the top. Immediately do one or two jog shuffles, retaining the six top cards. (If you can't do a Charlier, place the deck on the table and cut at the sides.)

Now, square the deck in preparation for a butt (faro) shuffle. As you do, give the deck a slight opposite-crimp bend, in order to get rid of the crimp. Do one butt shuffle, losing the top card. (This is an 'in' butt; the top card becomes second from top.)

The cut doesn't have to be even, and only the top six cards of each half have to interlace correctly. This places the selected card to twelfth from the top. Do another jog or two and place the deck, squared and face down, onto the table.

Remember please that the cuts to the crimp must be done without looking and without hesitation. Do the entire thing nonchalantly and as explained, and so far as anyone is concerned, the selected card is hopelessly lost.

Now say, "I'll make a very strong statement. I have no idea what or where your card is—but, if you name it, I'll spell it, whatever it is, from the top, without changing a single card!" Use the attitude here, that this is something that no other magician, in his right mind, would ever attempt.

Have him name his card. Repeat it and patter for a couple of seconds to give you time to figure out the spelling. Use one hand to slowly remove cards, one at a time, from the top, dropping them face down onto the table, as you spell the selected card. Turn up the card on the last letter or the next card, as circumstances demand, to end!

Afterthoughts:—Knowing that 'clubs' spells with five letters, 'hearts' and 'spades' with six letters, and 'diamonds' with eight—will help you to calculate quickly, just how to spell the selected card. For the 7S, for example, it's best to spell s-e-v-e-n, then say, "And it was spades, wasn't it?" And spell s-p-a-d-e-s; then turn over the next card.

There are only 17 cards where this is necessary—that is, omitting the 'of.' There are 28 cards (including the *deuce* of clubs) that are spelled, naturally, with 11 or 12 letters (15 cards with 12 letters and 13 cards with 11 letters). The remaining seven, I've already talked about.

It isn't necessary to memorize the amount of letters needed to spell every card. It's simple enough to work that out after the card is named, during a second or two of patter.

I just wanted to show you that the odds are the selected card will spell with 11 or 12 letters, which is perfect. And, as I said, I don't usually bother getting the exceptions to the top. The odds are against one of them being selected, and it doesn't matter to me, anyway.

For one of the club exceptions, I'd spell t-h-e s-i-x o-f, then I'd say, "And it was a club, wasn't it?" And I'd spell c-l-u-b. And turn the card on the last letter—'b.' For one of the diamonds, I'd spell s-e-v-e-n, then say, "And it's a diamond, right?" And spell d-i-a-m-o-n-d, again turning the card on the last letter—'d.'

Done nonchalantly and with authority, it just doesn't matter.

Please don't spell, say, a-c-e o-f c-l-u-b-s and then do a double-lift. You should *always* end with the deck on the table, and without any sleights.

The reason I spell the cards face down at the end, is that I don't want anyone to think I'm looking at the faces, perhaps to help me change my mode of spelling accordingly. Dealing the cards face down makes it appear much more *definite*.

One final point: Obviously, if a selected card is controlled to twelfth from the top in *any* manner, you can end the same way. As just one example; crimping *eleven* cards and eliminating the butt shuffle, would accomplish the same thing. But the trick would not be anywhere as good for a number of reasons. One of these reasons being that the butt helps to prove(?) that the deck is really shuffled.

I'll have to be immodest and tell you that after doing this for years, I know from experience that the way I've described it is the best way to handle it. Don't leave out the jog shuffles, incidentally.

Learn to do this well—I think you'll like its effect on your audiences.

THE FLIP-OVER LOCATOR

Handled correctly, this is a cute quickie. There's nothing particularly new in it, except perhaps the off-beat flip-over of a card. This flip-over is really the only reason for the effect in the first place. Without it, it's just a basic location of three cards.

Have three cards selected and apparently lost into a shuffled deck. You, of course, control them to the top. I *always* use my own 'Spread Control' for this. I described the Spread Control in *Close-Up Card Magic*, and again in *Personal Secrets*. I don't think it's necessary to describe it again.

If you don't already know it, I can only suggest that you look it up in either of the above-mentioned books, or use your 'favorite method' (and that's the first time I've ever used *that* phrase in a book!) to control three cards to the top of the deck.

After shuffling thoroughly, ask the first spectator to name his card. (The Spread Control brings the three cards to the top in 1, 2, 3 order. Therefore, the first spectator's card is on top. If you're using any other control, you ask the spectator whose card is on *top* to name his card at this point.)

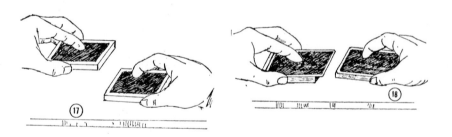

Now here's that flip-over which is really what makes this effect worthwhile. Cut the face down deck into two halves, as if you were about to do a table-top riffle shuffle. (See Fig. 17). The figure shows the cut almost completed. I think that in this instance, it isn't necessary for me to desrcibe the exact finger positions, etc. Just look at the figure, and you've got it.

The top half goes to the left and the lower half to the right. (In actual practice, the left hand moves the top half to the left while the right-hand half remains almost stationary.)

Do *not* release the lower half with the right fingers. As the cut is reaching completion, the left forefinger tip starts pushing the top card of the left-hand half to the right about half an inch. (See Fig. 18).

You must be sure that only *one* card moves here; the top card. If two cards move off, you'll ruin it. The best way to insure this is to use a good new deck, not an old sticky one.

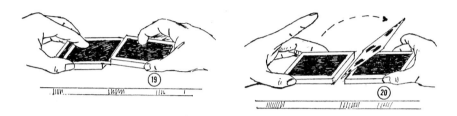

Place the left end of the right-hand half deck *onto* the protruding end of this card, so that there's about a quarter of an inch between the ends of the two half decks. The left forefinger keeps holding down the protruding top card. (See Fig. 19).

Now if you press down sharply with the right half deck and remove the left forefinger at the same time—the top card will flip over *onto* the right-hand half. (See Fig. 20). It will take perhaps, two or three tries for you to get the hang of this. (If you press down *too* sharply, the card may flip completely over the right-hand half. As I say, two or three tries and you'll get the knack.)

All right; this is the first spectator's card. Say, "Let's turn this 4S (or whatever it is) into a magic card. I'll leave it face up in the shuffled deck."

As you talk, grasp the two halves and start a table riffle shuffle. What you have to do is make sure that the face up card goes *between* the two top cards of the left-hand half. This is easy enough after a minimum of practice.

The way to do it is to allow all the cards to riffle off the right thumb until only the face up card remains. *Then* allow all the cards, but one, to riffle off the left thumb. (In other words, the right-hand half is riffled faster.) Then drop the face up card and finally, the last card of the left-hand half. (See Fig. 21). The thumbs have been moved back in the figure so that you can get an unobstructed view of the action.

Push the two halves into each other for only about an inch or so. Cut the deck at the sides while it's in this condition. (See Fig. 22). Complete the cut. Immediately spread the deck toward you (ribbon-wise) on the table, exposing the reversed card. (See Fig. 23).

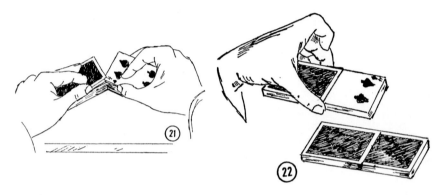

Of course, you can push the halves flush as soon as you riffle shuffle and *then* cut and spread, if you want to. I don't suggest it. Do it as I've explained. It looks better that way.

Now square the deck, push the halves flush, and say that the magic card will find the other two selected cards. Riffle the ends for effect and do a wide face down ribbon spread on the table, exposing that reversed card.

Remove the card on each side of the reversed card, holding one in each hand. Ask for the names of the two remaining selections; repeat the names and turn up the two cards you're holding—to end.

Afterthoughts:—I can't think of anything I can add to this. Just learn to do it smoothly; that is—after asking the name of the first spectator's card, the cutting, the flip-over, the riffle shuffle, the cut and spread—are all done in a blend of action, one leading into the other. Naturally, the three-card control must also be done well.

And then—you may get a kick out of performing this quickie.

FOURSOME

THERE are quite a few effects I would have included in one or the other of my books on card magic except that I felt they were too difficult to explain. They're the type of effects in which many different situations may present themselves while performing and I'd have to tell you what to do for each situation. This could, perhaps, take up more space than the effect is worth. I've decided, however, to include this one (also, "The Indicator," which is even more difficult to describe than this).

My good friend, Al Leech, started me thinking along these lines some years ago. The problem involves culling certain cards during one run-through of a shuffled deck. I don't think my method contains anything particularly new, but the routine is my own and it fools and impresses laymen—and magicians.

Effect, method and presentation:—Have a borrowed deck shuffled thoroughly. Try to spot the bottom card during the shuffle. If you can't, peek it as you take the deck or during your own riffle shuffle. Now shuffle that card to the top. In other words, you need a top key card *without* your spectator being aware of that fact.

Hold the deck in standard peek position, faces toward spectator. Run a fingertip from face to rear of deck, at the upper right-hand corner (See Fig. 24), as you ask him to stop you at any time. Be

sure he sees the card at which he stops you and tell him to remember it. Hold a break, as usual, with the flesh of the left little fingertip.

Now cut four packets to the table like this:—Cut half the cards from the top halfway to the break (about a quarter of the deck) to the table; cut up to the break and place on top of the tabled packet; cut half the remaining cards onto the tabled cards, and finally, drop all the remaining cards onto the deck.

Pick up the deck and slowly and obviously give it one complete cut. This cut should be made so that about twenty cards are brought from bottom to top. This will bring the thought-of card (and your key) to pretty near the top of the deck. (See Afterthoughts.)

Let me take a moment to explain this. Assuming the spectator stopped you originally somewhere near center, the selected card will be somewhere around 13th to 15th from the bottom after you've cut the four packets to the table. (It's your first cut that decides this, since the second cut has the selection at its face.)

I want the selection to be anywhere from, say, 5th to 10th from the top; so—that last cut of about twenty cards from bottom to top does this for me. And, I find that this last cut proves(?) I couldn't be controlling anything.

Although *any* control (or force) can be used for the selection, I always do it as just described. (See Afterthoughts.)

Okay; you now know that the selected card (and the key card) is somewhere near the top of the deck.

For this effect, starting now, I spread from my right hand to my left hand. This creates a bit of a problem, since I realize that most of you spread cards from your left to right hand. In all my writings up to now, when this problem arose, I simply transposed left and right. In this case, however, I think I can describe it better *exactly* as I do it, and let *you* do the transposing, if necessary.

At this point, I turn the deck face up, and quickly spread through once, saying, "Your card is somewhere in the deck. I couldn't possibly know where, or what, it is." The reason for this, is that I want to find out the name of the selected card. Since I know it is near the top (near bottom actually, since deck is face up), I don't have to search too long, and one split-second glance is all it takes.

So, I spot my original key and the card immediately above it is the selected card. (Really beneath it as you look at the cards; remember, the deck is face up. If you spread as I do, from right to left, the selection is to the right of the key; if you spread the other way—it's to the left.) Let's assume the selected card is the 7H.

Square the deck, keeping it face up. I patter to the effect that I can find the card only by elimination, and that I've learned to reduce the problem to only four cards. (I'd suggest you follow me from here on with deck in hand.)

I start spreading from right to left, allowing the spectator to see the faces of the cards just as I do. As soon as I see a 7-spot, *without hesitating*, I spread past it and square all the cards in my left hand. What I actually do here is tap the sides of the left-hand cards against the face of the right-hand cards in a squaring action. (See Fig. 25). I place the left-hand cards *face down*, onto the table, *as* my right thumb deals the face card of the right-hand cards, face up, onto the table. My attention is on the face up card my right hand is dealing.

What I've accomplished is: I have a small, face down, packet on the table to my left which has a seven on top. And on the table to my right, is a face up indifferent card. As I deal the indifferent card to the table, I say something like, "This *could* be your card."

Now I start spreading again. (The pause in spreading is only for a split second.) When I see another seven, I do *exactly* the same thing, except I do *not* place the left-hand cards to the table. I keep them where they are. My right hand deals the indifferent card face up onto the first one. I say, "Or *this* could be your card."

As I start to continue the spread, my left forefinger buckles the bottom one (the seven) of the left-hand cards. (See Fig. 26). I spread the right-hand cards *into* the space between this buckled card and the rest of the left-hand cards. (See Fig. 27).

As soon as I've started spreading into that space, I can relax my forefinger. The 7-spot will now automatically ride below the spread. I look for the third seven. When I see it, I do the exact same thing as before. This automatically leaves two sevens on top (at rear) of the left-hand cards. And I have three indifferent cards face up on the table.

Finally, I continue to spread the remaining right-hand cards, but now, I spread onto the *face* of the left-hand cards. When I come to the 7H, I do the same actions as before, and place *this* card onto the other three, making the same remark. And, I turn the cards in my hands face down after placing the remaining cards onto the face of the left-hand cards.

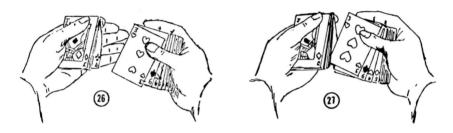

I've arrived at this position:—There are four face up cards on the table in front of me. The selected card (7H) is on top of the other three. There's a small face down packet on the table to my left with a 7-spot on top. The remaining cards are face down in my hand with two sevens on top.

And may I assure you that if this is done correctly, you cannot arouse any suspicions. It's all done during one fast spread-through, with no hesitations.

Now, the problem is to put the deck together (all but the four face up cards) bringing the three sevens, together, to the top. There are many ways to do it. I'll give you only one; the way I do it.

I hold the deck proper in my left hand. I pick up the tabled face down packet with my right, and place it on top of the left-hand cards, holding a little finger break.

The right fingers remove all the cards above the break, but the left thumb retains the top card. (See Fig. 28). Now, if you like, you can simply place this right-hand packet to the bottom, and you're set. I don't do that. I place the packet *back* on top, retaining the break. Now I double-cut (see "1-2-3 Aces" for a fast description) to the break. That's it. The three sevens are on top.

Now I do one or two jog shuffles, retaining the three top cards. I do all this (it takes just a second or two) as I look at the four tabled cards and patter to the effect that I think one of the four is the selected card, and so on.

All right; with my right hand, I use the selected card as a scoop to pick up the four tabled cards. This places the 7H to the rear of the four. And I place them *face up* onto the face down deck.

I spread them again (from left to right this time) saying, "I think that one of these, either the — of —, the — of —, the — of —, or the Seven of Hearts, is your card."

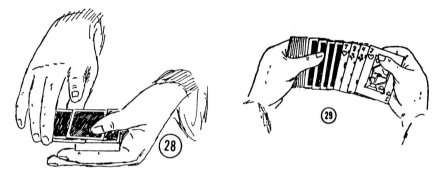

I spread three cards *past* the four face up cards (See Fig. 29), square and retain a break under all seven cards. From above, my right fingers pick up all cards (7) up to the break, and I do Braue's Add-On move, which is described in detail in *Close-Up Card Magic*, Page #50.

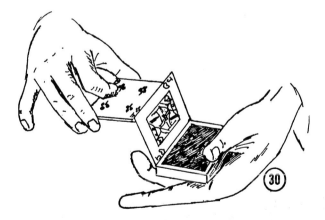

To keep this complete, here's a quick description: The left thumb slides the first face up card from the packet onto the deck proper and the packet itself is used as a lever to flip this card face down. (See Fig. 30).

Do this with three face up cards, then drop all remaining cards (spectators see only one face up card now) onto the deck; don't turn this card (7H) face down—leave it face up.

The patter as you do the add-on move: "At first I thought the — of — was your card, then I went to the — of —, then the — of —, finally, the Seven of Hearts."

Mention the name of each card as you bring it to the deck. Now, only the selected card (7H) is face up on top of the deck and the other three sevens are *directly under it*—the trick is done!

End like this:—Place the 7H face up onto the table, saying, "I finally decided that this is your card, not the — of —, the — of —, or the — of —." As you name the three cards, place the three top cards, face down, in a row beneath the 7H. Ask the spectator if you're correct. When he says that you are, say, "Well, I couldn't have gone *too* far wrong, because these are the other three sevens!" Turn the three sevens face up.

Afterthoughts:—If you learn this and do it correctly, you'll find that it's a stunner. Do it well, and your spectators will have *no* idea where the three matching cards come from. (Or, how you knew which was the selected card, for that matter.)

There are, of course, many ways you can start the effect other than the peek. This is up to you. One of my theories happens to be that I use certain moves or sleights for certain effects, *always*.

The logic behind this is that doing it exactly the same way all the time makes it second nature; I don't have to think about that part of the effect any more.

You can, however, use any control you like, or simply force the card. If you force it, there's no need for the first spread-through to find out what the card is. Although you'd have to spread and cut to get the card to near the top, anyway. Suffice it to say that I do it exactly as described.

The reason for getting the selection to near top, of course, is that the culling is easier if the three cards are culled before you reach the selection. Most of the time, if you do it as described, that will be the case.

Now we get into the area I mentioned about what to do for all circumstances. Well, I feel that those of you who can handle an effect of this kind will *know* what to do, no matter what. It just isn't worth taking the space to describe *all* possibilities.

Just one or two, however:—Say you're looking for the first seven and you come to *two* of them together. Great! This makes it easier. Simply do the same thing, getting the two sevens to the top of that first tabled packet. Then no buckle is necessary when you find the next (third) seven. The handling to get the sevens together on top is the same, except you'd reverse the packets. Just remember that the packet that has the one seven on top *goes* on top, so that you can slip-cut the seven to join the other two. (And don't make a surreptitious move out of this modified slip-cut. You're simply toying with the deck.)

If you come to two sevens together *after* you've culled the first one, again, it's easier. You simply eliminate the buckle. You're all set.

If you reach the selected card and still haven't culled the third seven, it doesn't matter. Simply place the selection to the table as usual—and keep going. You're supposedly looking for four cards, remember—so there's nothing illogical here. The only thing is, you won't have the selected card at the face of the four, after you've culled the last seven. So, either make sure the selection is protruding when you put it down, so that you can grab it for the scoop—or—simply pick up the *two* face cards and use them both to scoop. Just so the selected card winds up at the rear of the four.

I know that some of you will try to avoid the placing of the small packet to the table when you reach the first seven. You'll probably come to the conclusion that a *double* buckle would solve it. Well, I've already tried all ways, and another of my theories is that whenever I can avoid a sleight (or cover it) by doing a natural movement, I do so.

In this instance, I want to avoid any possible cause for hesitation. Placing this first packet to the table is a natural movement; and the double buckle *could* be a cause for hesitation.

I can only tell you that after playing with this for quite some time—I find my exact method to be the most natural and imperceptible way of culling the three cards.

The Add-On move (getting the three matching cards onto the three indifferent cards) is a standard move. I've added a forefinger lift-off which positively avoids the premature spreading of the cards. This is described in detail, as already mentioned, in *Close-Up Card Magic*.

Most important, learn to do this entire effect *without hesitation.* If your thinking shows at any time, you'll ruin it. Remember, you're simply looking for four cards—your attention is on *them, not* the cards you cull.

THE MAGIC STEP

T HIS IS something I've used, on and off, for some time. I never wrote it up before for one main reason—I didn't have a definite ending for it. Finally, I applied to this the idea I explained in *My Favorite Card Tricks* under "Transposition Breakthrough"—and it works just fine.

I originally used the routine for magicians only, because although the effect of a card changing is the same each time, the method is different for each one. And, I presented it with the attitude—"If you think you know what I'm doing, let me show it to you again." It was a 'challenge' type of thing and lost the magician somewhere along the way. With laymen, of course, there's no problem at all—they should be fooled right down the line.

I'd suggest you follow me with cards in hand, and although the push-down move is one with which you're most likely familiar—pay close attention to every gesture and the presentation in general.

After the deck has been shuffled, square it and hold it face down in the left hand, up near the fingertips—thumb on one long side,

forefinger curled beneath and the remaining fingers at the opposite side. The deck is held vertically, facing the spectator.

Reach over with the right hand, and grasping the deck from above, with thumb at inner end and fingers at the other end, push (or lift) the *top half up* about five-eighths of an inch. (See Fig. 31).

Remove the right hand. The patter during this is, "When I form this magic step with a deck of cards, strange things happen. Watch."

The right hand approaches and double-lifts from the top of the stepped-up half. This, I'm sure, is no problem for you. If it is, see my "Ambitious Card Routine" in *Close-Up Card Magic,* where I describe a double-lift that fits in here perfectly.

Display and replace the card(s). Take off the top card, repeating the name of the card displayed, and push it between the top half and lower half. (See Fig. 32). Finish pushing it flush (with the lower half) with the ball of the right thumb. (See Fig. 33). Tap it with your right forefinger, saying, "There's the — of —."

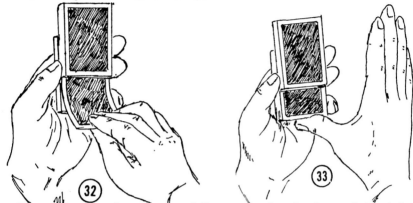

The right thumb and second fingertip take the *lower half* of the lower half, at the inner corners. (See Fig. 34) This packet is going to be placed onto the stepped-up top half. But pause as it's being carried there to tap the top of the exposed lower half with the right forefinger, and say, "Remember, here's the — of —." (See Fig. 35). Now deposit the packet onto the stepped-up top half.

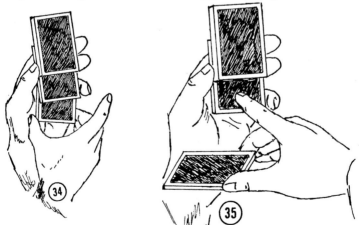

The right hand returns to grasp the remainder of the lower half in the same manner, in order to carry *it* onto the top half. But again, as you carry it there, pause to indicate its top card with the right forefinger tip, and mention the card's name. (See Fig. 36).

Snap your fingers and show the top card. It has changed, of course. I've described this in detail because this same action is used two more times. Although I've broken it down into steps, it should be done in a blend of movement.

Patter:—"Perhaps you think you know what happened here. Well, whether you do or not, I'll repeat it for you." Step the deck as before and this time, actually show the top card only of the top half. If you're working for another magician, make this quite obvious.

Place this card to the top of the lower half just as before. Start to push it flush with the right thumb. Now here's the move. The left forefinger nail (if you bite your nails, you're in trouble) rests on the top edge of the face card of the top half. The right thumb pushes the displayed card until it's about five-eighths of an inch from being flush. (Refer back to Fig. 33).

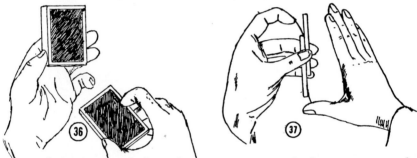

At this point, and this takes some practice before acquiring the 'knack'—snap the card the rest of the way home as *at the same exact moment,* the left forefinger snaps a card (or more) downward. (See Fig. 37), for a sideways view of this action—about mid-way.

If the right thumb and left forefinger move at the same speed (this must be a snap movement), it's impossible to see the card coming down over the displayed card. Of course, it must be done neatly. Try doing it without thinking and with confidence—and you'll surprise yourself. (It's a bit easier to hide this using a deck with no margins, such as a Bee back deck—but if it's done correctly, it doesn't matter.)

Don't be afraid to *snap* these cards. The inner end of the lower half deck acts as a 'stop' for the right thumb and the outer end does the same for the left forefinger tip.

All right; now finish *exactly* as described for the first change. Don't omit indicating the displayed(?) card with the right forefinger, just as I explained. End as before, showing that the card has changed.

"Well, I don't know if you have any idea of what I'm doing, but I'll give you another chance."

Start exactly the same way, showing a single card. Put it between the halves and push it flush with the right thumb. This time, do it slowly and obviously. Don't say anything about this; just do it.

Do the first part—taking the bottom half of the lower half and bringing it to the top. Don't forget to indicate the displayed card with the right forefinger tip.

Now, *as* the right hand places this packet onto the top, the left forefinger tip does the same push-down move as in the preceding change. Except that this time, there's no need to snap it. Do it in a smooth, easy motion. There must be no hesitation here. The right hand pauses only long enough to place its packet to the top. That's *all* the time you need to push down with the left forefinger tip. (You can start the move *before* the right hand actually deposits its packet.)

The right hand is perfect cover for the card moving down over the displayed card. (See Fig. 38) for sideways view. Done neatly, this will fool anyone! Finish as in the preceding changes.

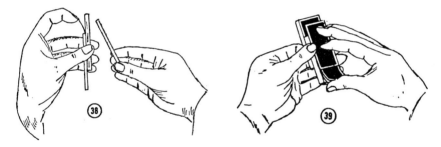

Now for the ending I mentioned. As I've told you, this is the effect I described under the title, "Lorayne's Transposition Breakthrough #1" in *My Favorite Card Tricks*. I'd suggest you look it up, because it's described in minute detail there.

Patter:—"Up to now, I've stepped the deck *upward*; if I step it downward, even stranger things happen. Watch."

Hold the deck as you have been, but horizontally this time, and step the top half downward. Double-lift from the top half, displaying the card. (Let's assume it's the 7C). Replace, and push forward the top card (only), about half an inch, saying, "I'll even push the 7C forward so you can keep your eye on it."

Now, double-lift the two cards *under* this protruding card. (See Fig. 39). Display the card. (Assume it's the 6D.) Replace the card(s) flush *onto* the stepped-down top half (onto the pushed-forward card). The first card (supposedly the 7C) is still protruding.

Point to this protruding card, saying, "Remember, here's the 7C." Point to the top card, "And here's the 6D on top of it." Push the protruding card flush, slowly. "You have to remember that the 6D is on top with the 7C directly beneath it." Be sure your spectators remember which is which.

Take off the top card, calling it the 6D, and push it via the outer end, between the two halves, flush with the lower half. (See Fig. 40). Explain that now the 6D is on top of the lower half and the 7C is on top of the top half. Indicate each one as you mention it.

Ask the spectator to tell you which is which. When he does, say, "Right. But watch." Snap your fingers, or what have you, and show that the two cards have changed places. That's the end.

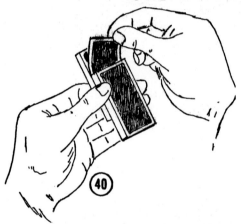

This last, of course, works automatically if you follow my instructions exactly. I can only repeat my suggestion that you check this in *My Favorite Card Tricks*, if you feel it's not described fully enough here. I didn't think it would be fair to take all that space again. But I did want to give at least a quick description, just to keep this complete unto itself.

Afterthoughts:—You do, of course, have to watch your angles. The backs of the cards should be facing your audience. Certainly, you can't allow anyone behind you. The deck is held vertically rather than horizontally for all except the ending.

Be assured that you'll fool people with this routine, *if* you do it neatly and well. My wife, Renée, who is the *toughest* person for me to fool (she usually knows what I'm going to do *before* I do it—

with *cards,* that is)—said that the only thing she *felt* I was doing, was the double-lift. Other than that, she was completely fooled.

I don't *expect* to fool my wife or another magician with a double-lift. But that's the whole point of this. That's what made me evolve this routine. I wanted to make the magician think he knew exactly what I was doing, and then fool him! No problem with laymen, of course.

Try this; practice it; I'm partial enough to think that you may like it.

NEW-FANGLED COLOR CHANGE

I'M ASSUMING (wrongly, I hope) that most of you won't even try this. Those of you who do, will find it easy to do and a fooler, to boot.

I realize that there are more than enough good color changes in existence—but, you may want to use this to fool other magicians.

I'll teach you the basic move and then give you some ideas on how to use it. I suggest you read this with cards in hand. I'll let the illustrations do most of the work for me.

Hold the deck face up in the left hand, up near the fingertips. The face of the deck is toward your spectator. Turn toward your left a bit, so that your right side is more to the front. Left thumb is at the center of one long side; first, second, third and fourth fingers on the opposite long side (or forefinger bent at rear of deck). (See Fig. 41).

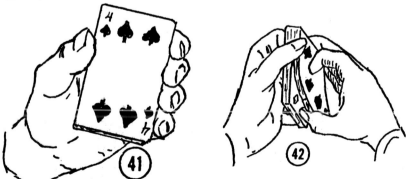

The right hand approaches and breaks away a small packet of cards, say about fifteen, from the face of the deck. (See Fig. 42). The left hand does not change position; the remaining cards (the deck proper) are grasped firmly.

The right hand executes a one-hand fan with its small batch of cards, faces toward spectator. (See Fig. 43). Turn both hands over once or twice to show that nothing is concealed, etc.

Now; call attention to the face card of those in the left hand. Approach the squared left-hand cards with the right-hand fan. As you get close, *extend the right first and fourth fingers* as far as you can! You'll find that you can extend these two fingers straight out without disturbing the fan. It will feel a bit awkward at first, and may take a try or two, but it's really easy. (See Fig. 44).

Okay; if you tilt the left-hand cards slightly forward, you'll find that you can grasp the face card (or cards) by the *ends* with the sides of the tips of the extended right first and fourth fingers. (See Fig. 45).

Grasp this card—and with a minimum of practice, you'll do it almost instantaneously, although there's no need to rush—and move the right hand downward. (See Fig. 46). As you do, straighten out the tilt of the left-hand cards. It appears as if you're simply brushing the face card with the right-hand fan.

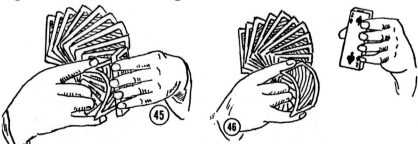

You'll notice that the card you stole will buckle slightly—that's okay; don't worry about it.

That's the basic move. With proper attention to angles, it's a startling change. Always do it *below* your spectator's eye level, and always tilt the left-hand cards slightly forward as you steal. That way, the fan of cards in your right hand will hide all the dirty work.

The left fingers hold the deck proper *firmly*, so that no cards move except the one you steal. After some practice, you'll be able to steal one, two or three, or more, cards by feel. In a moment, you'll see where you may want to steal more than one card.

Now then, you've done the change but you're left holding a card (or cards) between your extended right first and fourth fingers. This card can be replaced just as easily as you removed it. In other words, repeat the exact actions of brushing the left-hand cards with the fan and replace the card as you do.

But—although replacing the card is all right, it may tend to *tell* other magicians that you are removing a card somehow and then simply replacing it; it will give them a starting point for reconstructing it. If you *want* to do it that way, you'll find that as you move the fan *up* along the face of the left-hand cards (in order to move down again) the tip of the right fourth finger will act as a 'stop' when it reaches the lower end of the deck proper. Now you can replace the card perfectly flush and its re-appearance is as startling as its disappearance. Then, be sure to close the right first and fourth fingers again; show all sides of both hands; square all the cards— and that's it.

If you want to do the change *without* replacing the stolen card, do this:—Bring the left-hand cards to the right-hand fan (actually, both hands should move toward each other); replace the stolen card as the left hand *keeps moving* until it is holding its cards *face down*. The right hand keeps moving until the face up fan is horizontal to the floor. (See Fig. 47).

This is all done in one fluid motion. You're simply displaying both sides of the cards in each hand. Because, now you turn the fan face down and place it to the bottom of the deck proper. Square the deck and that's it.

In this way, the card that was originally changed is not seen again. All this is difficult to describe, but I'm sure you'll get it after a few tries. It can be done in less than a second after a bit of practice. Remember to always close the right first and fourth fingers as soon as you've replaced the card. If you leave them extended when you turn the hand over, not only will it appear as if you're giving someone the sign of the 'evil eye,' but it will also 'tip' the secret.

Now; one or two other ways of doing this change:—You can steal a small group of cards instead of only one card. If you do that, you can do two or three changes in a row. The first change is when you steal. Then as you brush with the fan again, replace the cards and *re-steal* a *smaller group* in the same movement!

Then repeat! You can end by getting back to the original card by simply replacing it during the last brushing (by this time, your spectator will probably have forgotten that it was the original card); or end as I've explained so that you *don't* show that card again.

Finally, here's a way of using this for a double color change. Holding the deck in the left hand as already described, approach with the right fingers and step up (about an inch) about *two-thirds* of the deck. (Just as in 'The Magic Step,' except face up, here.)

Now break off a packet of cards from the face of this stepped-up two-thirds and do a one-hand fan with them. (See Fig. 48) You're in position to do the color change as before, except that the deck proper is in stepped position with *two cards* visible.

You're also in the exact position to push down the *rear* card (or cards) of the stepped-up packet so that that card covers the face card of the lower packet. This card is pushed down with the tip of the left forefinger, remember—just as in 'The Magic Step.'

All right; call attention to the two visible cards and start to brush with the right-hand fan. *As* you steal the face card of the stepped-up packet (this is no problem incidentally. Just ignore the lower packet. As a matter of fact, the right fourth fingertip rests against this packet as you steal; it gives you leverage) push down a card.

It appears as if one brush of the fan has changed both cards! (See Fig. 49) for an exposed view of all the action.

Now you can repeat the double change by replacing the stolen card and pushing down another card with the left forefinger. Or — — end as already explained.

Incidentally, you may feel that it's easier to start as for a single change and *then* push half the deck down with the left forefinger in order to step the deck. Well, it may be easier, but don't do it! If you do, you'll be spotlighting the fact that you *can* push down cards this way to change the face card of the lower packet. Although magicians may know this move, they'll be thrown by the change of the other face card, and shouldn't be able to reconstruct it.

Try these changes and you'll see how simple they are. There are, of course, other color changes using a fan of cards, in a brushing motion, as the cover. In most of them, however, you *must* brush at least *twice* in order to do the change—because in most of them, a card must be stolen *first* (usually from the rear of the deck) and *then* placed on the face card.

Of course, when doing this for a layman, you can brush once or twice for effect, before you steal. But for a magician, explain about usually having to cover the face card twice, etc.—and show that *you* do it by brushing only *once*. Try it—you'll fool him!

Afterthoughts:—This has been difficult to describe, but with the illustrations, which show exact positions of cards and fingers, you should get it after a few tries.

Remember to watch your angles and to tilt the deck slightly forward as you steal the card. Then tilt back again as you brush down with the fan.

If you have small hands as I do, you'll find that at first, you may have to strain just a bit in order for your extended first and fourth fingers to spread far enough apart to grasp the card.

After a while, this will come easier and easier, but as an aid right now—simply allow the right fourth fingertip to rest on the bottom of the lower end of the deck proper. Now if you keep moving the right hand upward, keeping the fourth finger there (using that lower end as leverage) your fingers will automatically spread further apart. (See Fig. 50).

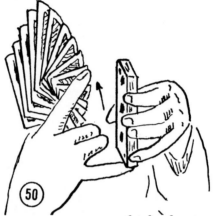

Incidentally, you may want to think about using the double change as an ending for 'The Magic Step' instead of the ending I taught you there. With proper patter, it would fit perfectly.

Although I never use it this way, but for completion's sake:— You can avoid having to stretch your first and fourth fingers too far apart by holding the deck at the *ends* originally instead of the sides. You would do it in exactly the same way, except that the deck proper would be held horizontally instead of vertically. I don't suggest you do it this way, however—it may be too obvious.

I started doing this change for magicians just as a gag. I found that it fooled them. I polished it up a bit, and I've used it ever since. Practice a while; I think you'll have fun with it.

OUTRAGEOUS REVELATION

THIS IS another thing I started to do as a gag for other magicians. No one was more surprised than I, when it fooled them.

This, I think, will be the shortest description of a trick that I've ever written. The effect is simply this:—A card is selected and shuffled into the deck. You carry the face down deck under the table top and *instantaneously* bring it back again. The selected card appears face up on top!

You must be seated at a table as you control the selected card to the top. Now reverse it so that it is face up *second* from the top. There are many ways to do this; I explained a few methods in *Close-Up Card Magic.*

The easiest (though not necessarily the best) way is to double-lift, leaving the card(s) face up on top as you ask if this is the selected card. Turn the deck face up, asking if the face card is the selection. Still holding the deck face up, pull out the (now) bottom card, turn it face up (See Fig. 51) and stress that neither top nor

bottom card is the selected one. Replace this card face up (as the rest of deck) to bottom. Turn the deck face down—and the selected card is face up second from top. Or—use the method I explain for the four aces (using one card only, of course) in "1-2-3 Aces."

You must get into this position without anyone being the wiser. I always jog shuffle once or twice after the card is set. Now hold the deck squared and turn it face up for a moment so that everyone sees that the selected card is not at the bottom.

Holding the deck face down in dealing position, ask for the name of the card. Now—with your dealing hand only (holding the deck), go under the table and immediately *deal off the top card.* Just let it fall to the floor—*don't* try to lap it.

And, *instantaneously*, bring the deck back into view; the selected card is face up on top! Leave the deck on the table—and the trick is over!

Afterthoughts:—Don't knock this until you try it! I can only tell you that I've fooled groups of magicians with it, time and again.

The reason for showing the bottom card is that there is a method of accomplishing this by bringing the face card over onto the top with the thumb. Showing the face card will fool the magicians who know this. And anyway—there's *no* method that can accomplish this *as quickly!*

You *must* go under the table top and come back *instantaneously.* You can start dealing off the top card *as* you go under, then come back without actually stopping.

Trying to lap the card will cause a moment's hesitation and more important, it necessitates angle-watching; dealing it to the floor usually doesn't.

Finally, do *not* pick up the dropped card, for goodness' sake! Just forget it. Later on, you can either drop some other cards and pick up the original one with them, or—pretend to see it suddenly and simply remark that *someone* dropped a card, as you nonchalantly pick it up.

Or—if you don't need a complete deck for other tricks, as I said, just forget it! It's up to you.

OUTRAGEOUS REVELATION #2

H ERE's another bare-faced swindle you may want to try. Although you may not think it from reading it—I've fooled magicians with this, time and again. This will be an even shorter description than the preceding.

The effect is the instant reversal of a selected card. It couldn't be more 'instant' since the spectator himself replaces his card already reversed. Here's how:—

You're seated at a table opposite your spectator. Have him shuffle the deck and then hand it to you under the table. Spread the deck for the selection of a card. All this is done *under the table.*

The moment he removes a card, and as you tell him to look at and remember it—turn the deck *face up* and immediately spread it again. The idea here is that I want the spectator to feel the deck still in spread condition when he replaces his card.

Rush him after the selection. Tell him to just look at his card while it's still under the table—not to bring it all the way out. This way it appears as if there couldn't be enough time for you to do *anything.* Don't mention this, however.

He replaces his card, under the table, and you push the deck, as is, into his hands and tell him to shuffle thoroughly, under the table. When he's shuffled, he hands the deck back to you—still under the table.

You give it another loud riffle shuffle or two, turn it face down, and bring it into view. As you do, glance at it to make sure that the face up card is *not* on top. (If it should happen to be—just give the deck a cut before bringing it out, or—lap the card, and end accordingly.)

Ask for the name of the selected card, make your magic gesture, and do a wide face down ribbon spread, showing the chosen card reversed!

Afterthoughts:—I always go right into another trick after I've done this—so as not to give my spectator any time to think about it! (You might, for example, say that you can reverse any card he selects, and do 'Toss-In Reverse' from *My Favorite Card Tricks,* 'Four Of A Kind' from *Personal Secrets,* or 'Two Card Reverse' from *Close-Up Card Magic.*)

Do this thing just as I've explained and you'll probably fool other magicians. I don't know—maybe the reason I've fooled magicians with it, is that they didn't believe I'd stoop so low as to do a silly thing like this!

THAT BURNS ME UP!

THIS IS just a crazy off-beat idea for a quick lit cigarette effect. It's performed while standing and takes just a few seconds. I use it as a 'throw-away' type of thing.

Before starting, be sure to have some loose change in your right outside jacket pocket. If that pocket has a flap, push the flap into the pocket in order to avoid trouble with it later.

Hold a lit cigarette in your right hand. Now do any move during which it appears as if you're putting the cigarette into your left hand, but it is retained in the right hand. The standard cigarette thumb palm will do. Or, the simplest way and the one I usually use:—Hold the cigarette between the right thumb and fingers, lit end down, as in (Fig. 52).

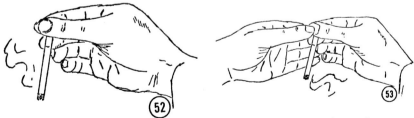

Approach the left hand with your right as if to place the cigarette there. The left fingers cover the right fingers as if taking the cigarette. (See Fig. 53). Move the left hand away, keeping it in position as if it were holding the cigarette. The right hand remains momentarily stationary, but the second fingertip bends in, tilting the cigarette slightly to the right. This takes it out of sight; the right hand covering it completely. (See Fig. 54). This is done, of course, as the left hand pretends to take the cigarette. It's all done in one fluid action, and your eyes follow the left hand. (The most basic

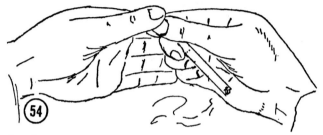

misdirection.)

As you do the move, say, "I'm sure you've seen magicians do the trick where they put a lit cigarette in one hand, then produce it with the other hand. I don't do that. When I make it disappear, I usually produce it from my pocket . . ."

Suit action to words. As you mention placing the cigarette in one hand—do the move. As you talk about producing it from your pocket, open the left hand (after blowing on it, or rubbing the fingers, if you like) to show it empty; *at the same time,* go into your jacket pocket with the right hand.

The left hand now goes into your left jacket pocket. As soon as your right hand is in the pocket, let the cigarette fall momentarily onto the curled right fingers (it won't burn you, I assure you). Now gently drop the cigarette flat onto the coins in the pocket, and immediately withdraw your hand. Bring out your left hand at the same time. All this takes about one second.

Keep both hands in motion (they're wide open, fingers spread) as they go in and out of different pockets, looking for the cigarette. The patter, "Now wait a minute; didn't I just have a cigarette?"

The secret here (besides a little nerve) is to keep both your hands *and* your jacket in motion. The buttons should be open so that you can open the jacket wide once or twice as you apparently search for the cigarette. The coins tend to absorb the heat and protect the pocket; and the jacket moving keeps the cigarette moving, so that it doesn't stay in one place and start trouble.

After a few seconds, both hands go into the outside jacket pockets. The right hand retrieves the cigarette by holding it loosely on the curled fingers. Clip the unlit end between the thumb and fore finger tips. You'll find that it's safe to hold it that way and also, that it's completely hidden by the fingers. Although it doesn't really matter whether it's completely hidden or not.

The left hand opens the left side of your jacket as the right hand moves from your pocket and reaches into this opening. Bring the hand right out again with the cigarette at the fingertips.

Puff on it to show that it's lit, and say, "Oh yes, I forgot; I always keep it right here!"

Afterthoughts:—Some points to keep in mind: Act as if you really don't know where the cigarette is as you search for it. Keep the hands and jacket in motion throughout.

Don't use too short a butt. It's easier to handle a longer one. Don't attempt it with a badly lit cigarette. If the lit end is loose, it may fall off in your pocket! I know this from experience. It happened to me while lecturing to a roomful of magicians; but that's the *only* (and last) time it ever happened. Just be sure that the cigarette is normally well-lit.

If you're nervous after performing, nonchalantly jingle the coins in your right pocket; that will extinguish any live ash. And do this entire thing in an off-hand manner, as if you just thought of it.

The longer the cigarette is in the pocket, the more you'll fool people. It takes some nerve, admittedly, but you realize, of course, that you'll fool people *because* nobody would expect you to leave a lighted cigarette in your pocket for *any* length of time. (The same holds true for *sleeving* a lighted cigarette, which I've used for years.)

One final point: If ever anyone mentions that he thinks you may have left the cigarette in your pocket, smile knowingly and say, "Sure I did!" Let him think about it—you can be sure he'll never try it. Don't admit it, whatever you do!

THE CARD PYRAMID

M Y FRIEND, T. A. Waters, started me thinking along these lines when he showed me an interesting stunt with numbers. He showed me how it worked and that was the end of it; or so I thought. I don't usually go overboard for *just* number stunts, unless I can apply the idea to something else which I feel is entertaining to laymen.

Well, this mathematical idea rambled round and round in my brain until I got the simple thought that laying out playing cards instead of numbers might be just the thing. I worked on presentation for a while and then I tried it out. I've used it ever since and it seems to be interesting, intriguing and entertaining to everyone who sees it.

Martin Gardner, who by coincidence was contemplating doing a column for Scientific American magazine on Pascal's triangle (on which this is based), heard about it and asked me if he could include my idea of using cards. So if this appears vaguely familiar to you, you may have read his monthly column, Mathematical Games, in the Dec., 1966 or Jan., 1967 issues of Scientific American.

Of course, he wasn't writing for magicians, and didn't include any presentation at all. I've also added a 'kicker' to this that will drive mathematicians 'up the wall.'

Effect, method and presentation:—From an ordinary deck, openly remove all the tens, jacks, queens and kings. Put these 16 cards aside; you'll use the aces to nines only for this. As you're removing these cards, ask your spectator if he knows how to form a card pyramid.

When he says, "No" (which he will, since he has no idea what a card pyramid *is*), lay five cards onto the table in a face up horizontal row. They should not overlap; leave them about a quarter inch apart. Assume you've put down a 5, 7, 2, 4 and an ace, from left to right. (See Fig. 55).

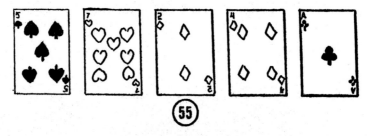

(55)

Explain to the spectator that what has to be done is to add *each* pair of cards down to a single digit. Point to the 5 and the 7 and explain that these two cards total 12, but since that isn't a single digit, he would add the 1 and the 2 (of the 12), arriving at 3. (What's actually happening is—you're casting out nines and arriving at the digital root.)

Then he'd find a 3-spot in the deck and place it above and be-

tween the two cards he's added. Then he'd add the next pair, the
7 and 2 in our example, to get 9, a single digit. He'd find a 9-spot
and place it between and above the 7 and 2. Then the 2 and 4 are
added to get 6, etc. (See Fig. 56). After completing this first row,
he works on the newly-formed row; and he's to keep doing this
until he gets to the apex (top single card) of the pyramid. By this
time (or sooner), after demonstrating with one or two cards, he'll
know just what you mean; if he doesn't, you shouldn't be doing this
kind of stunt for him in the first place!

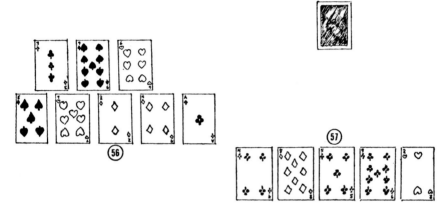

All right; pick up all the cards you've used in the example. Give
your spectator all the cards from aces to nines and tell him to
shuffle. Then tell him to put down, in a face up row, as you've
demonstrated, any five cards. He can change his mind, or the cards,
as often as he likes. And after he has the cards down, tell him that
he can shift them around any way he likes.

When he's satisfied, you take the remaining cards and say that
you want to make a prediction. You take out a card and place it
face down above his five face up cards, at the position you judge
the apex card of the pyramid will fall. (See Fig. 57).

Now we come to the heart of the matter. How do you know
which card to put down as your prediction? Without getting into
the whys and wherefores of this, here's the formula that's applied
to the five face up cards:—1, 4, 6, 4, 1.

This is easy enough to remember, and what the digits mean is
that you *multiply* the first card by 1; the second card by 4; the third
(center) card by 6; the fourth card by 4, and the last card by 1.
You *add* the answers to each other and *cast out all nines* as you
move along.

Don't get panicky! There's nothing to it. First of all, I'm sure
you know that in order to 'cast out the nines' from any number
(we're concerned with two-digit numbers only for this) you simply
add the digits until you're left with only one digit. A few examples:—To cast out the 9s from 16, add the 1 and 6 to get 7; 13 = 4;
18 = 9 (which is 0 — cast out *all* the 9s); 11 = 2; 17 = 8; 20 = 2;
32 = 5; 48 = 12 = 3, etc.

Okay; let's use the five cards in the last figure (4, 8, 5, 9, 2) as
an example, and I'll try to explain just how my mind works. Multiplying by 1 means that the number is left *as is*. So, I simply add
the two end cards (4 and 2) and keep 6 in mind. Now, multiplying
the 8 by 4 produces 32; casting out the 9s (3 + 2) gives me 5. I
add this 5 to the 6 already in mind, getting 11, but immediately
cast out 9, leaving me to work with 2.

Going to the card second from the right (the 9), I see that I
can ignore this completely. Because, multiplying 9 by *anything* and
then casting out the 9s, will bring you to zero. (9 × 4 = 36; 3 + 6
= 9; 9 = 0.) So, in calculating for this effect, you *always* ignore
9-spots.

I'm still working with 2. Now, multiplying the center card (5)
by 6, results in 30; I think 3 (3 + 0). Adding this 3 to the 2 I'm
carrying, gives me 5. *That's* what I predict; 5. And if you work out
the pyramid with the 4, 8, 5, 9 and 2, you'll see that it does reach
its apex with a 5. (See Fig. 58).

(58)

It takes much longer to explain this than to do it. Try it once
or twice and you'll have it. I nearly always work it as explained.
Add the two end cards; then multiply the next-to-last cards at each
end by 4; and finally, multiply the center card by 6.

I've already told you to ignore any 9-spot; and, if you see a 3 or a 6 as the center card, you can ignore that too; because 3 or 6 times 6 will come out to zero. ($3 \times 6 = 18 = 9 = 0$; $6 \times 6 = 36 = 9 = 0$.)

This is all in the interest of working quickly. After performing this for a short while, I was able to do all the calculating by the time I took the cards from the spectator, and supposedly searched for the card I wanted.

To make sure you understand this, let's go through one more example. Say the cards put on the table are an 8, 3, ace, 7, 6. Okay; immediately add the 8 and 6 (end cards) to get 14, and think 5. Multiply the 3-spot by 4 to get 12, and think 3. 5 + 3 is 8. Multiply the 7-spot by 4 to get 28 (which is 10; 2 + 8), and think 1. Adding this 1 to the 8 gives you 9—which is dropped. All that remains is to multiply the ace by 6, which *is* 6—and that's the prediction. (See Fig. 59). (See Afterthoughts for another good shortcut idea.)

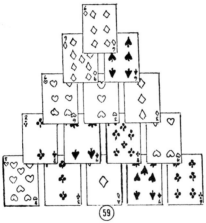

(59)

Now for some presentation pointers. As the spectator is forming the pyramid, help him with the additions and of course, make sure he does them correctly. As the pyramid grows, try to judge if your prediction card will fall just at apex position. If you think not, just reach over and adjust it—shift it lower, higher, or what have you.

When he reaches the point where he adds just the last two cards (in the last figure, the 9 and 6) to get the apex 6, let him start to look for it, and then say, "Here, I'll save you the trouble of looking for a 6, because that's the card I predicted." As you say this, turn over your prediction card and place it in position as the apex of the pyramid, to end.

Sometimes, a situation may arise where the spectator runs out of a particular card. In such a case, tell him to use any picture card and simply let it represent the spot card (number) he needs.

Usually, however, if he does run out of a particular card, it will be the apex card. That's just fine for the ending. Let him look for the card until he either says he can't find one or looks at you in confusion. Then say, "Of course you can't find it; it isn't there. That's the card I predicted!" (The last example I used falls into this category. See the last figure and you'll note that the apex 6-spot is the last of the four sixes.)

Well, that's about it for the basic effect. I always do it at least twice; one reason being that I don't want it to look like a lucky guess, and also, sometimes the digital root of the original five cards (totaling and casting out the 9s) will match your prediction. (3, 1, 6, 7, 5 is an example of this.) This is coincidental, of course, but someone who knows about casting out 9s may think that's the answer. So I would definitely repeat it to prove that it is not.

All right; you can do it a few times and quit, or, end with the 'kicker' I mentioned. It will take a little work, or preparation, on your part, to be able to do this. But once you've prepared, you'll be prepared and ready, to do it at any time.

The effect is that you do the card pyramid *backwards.* In other words, you tell the spectator that you'll let *him* predict the apex card of the pyramid. You let him pull any card out of a face down spread and place it face up in apex position. You pick up the cards and remove five, which you place face up in a horizontal row, as the first row of the pyramid!

Let him take the deck and complete the pyramid, and of course, it works out correctly to fit the apex card he originally selected!

Doing the card pyramid the regular way—when *you* predict the apex—is tough enough to figure out, although someone well-versed in mathematics would eventually do it, I guess. Presented properly, it's just about impossible for a mathematician to figure out this 'kicker' for the simple reason that it has nothing to do with mathematics! (See Afterthoughts for a mathematical method.)

What it has to do with is something quite familiar to me, and that's—*memory.* I guess you've got it now, haven't you? All that's necessary, is to memorize a five-digit number for each digit from 1 to 9. That is—nine five-digit numbers. Each of the five-digit numbers, of course, will represent the five cards that form a pyramid ending with the digit you've connected it with in your memory.

As you probably know, memorizing these nine five-digit numbers is no problem for me. If it is for you, I can only suggest that you pick up a copy of my book, *How To Develop A Super-Power Memory*, or any of my other books on the subject. It's simple enough when you know how!

More than one combination of five-digit numbers can fit any of the digits from 1 to 9, but all you have to memorize is one combination (of five digits) for each. Here's the list I use:—

$$1 - 84258$$
$$2 - 28761$$
$$3 - 46971$$
$$4 - 19324$$
$$5 - 75311$$
$$6 - 59234$$
$$7 - 95156$$
$$8 - 64837$$
$$9 - 36827$$

It took quite a while to compile this list, because I had three stipulations. I didn't want *any* similar pairs of numbers, which might confuse the memory work. I didn't want any of the combinations to use more than four of a kind in forming the pyramid, so that the spectator wouldn't have to use a picture card as a substitute. And—I didn't want any of the five-digit numbers, after totaling and casting out the 9s, to match the apex card. If you check, you'll see that all the combinations meet all three stipulations or conditions.

So, there it is. If the spectator should select a 6-spot for his 'prediction' (the apex card)—you'd put down the following cards: 5, 9, 2, 3 and a 4.

The important thing is to act this out as if it were based on mathematics. I'll leave this to you. Don't take the five cards out immediately. Make it appear as if you're doing *some* calculations.

You see, when you're actually *doing* some calculations (for the regular pyramid), you should try to make it appear as if you are *not* doing any, and can immediately take out your prediction card. When you're *not* doing any calculations, you should try to make it appear as if you are! Sneaky, eh?

Afterthoughts:—I think I've just about covered everything; there isn't anything more I can tell you about the presentation.

So far as calculating the apex for the regular pyramid is concerned—after a while, you'll be able to do it at (almost) a glance.

You'll get to *know* what certain cards break down to when they're in certain positions.

What I mean is—after doing this for a while, you'll know that an 8-spot in second-from-either-end position means — 5. (8 $\times$ 4 = 32 = 5.) A 4-spot in either of those positions means — 7; a 4-spot in center position means 6 (4 $\times$ 6 = 24 = 6). And so on.

With practice and experience, it really boils down to simply adding single digits and casting out the 9s the shortcut way, as I explained in the text.

Here's a handy shortcut, which I'm sure you'd have thought of eventually. Since the two next-to-last cards are both multiplied by 4 — you can simply add the two cards (casting out 9s, if necessary) and multiply the *answer* by 4. This cuts the two multiplying steps to one.

Example:—If the two next-to-last cards were an 8 and a 7, you'd add them to get 15, which equals 6. 4 $\times$ 6 = 24 = 6. If the two cards are a 7 and 6, add them to get 13, or 4. 4 $\times$ 4 = 16 = 7. If the cards are a 2 and 5 — multiply 7 by 4 to get 28, or 10, or 1. You'll find that this will help you to cut your calculation time way down. (And it comes in very handy for the mathematical method of doing my 'kicker,' as you'll see in a moment.)

If you don't want to memorize the nine five-digit numbers for the 'kicker' as I described, I can make it much easier for you. It's easier, but not as good. Here's what I mean:—You can memorize the number, 84258, which is the combination for #1, and by simply changing the last digit, you'd have the combination for #2 to #9. Look:—

$$84258 = 1$$
$$84259 = 2$$
$$84251 = 3$$
$$84252 = 4$$
$$84253 = 5$$
$$84254 = 6$$
$$84255 = 7$$
$$84256 = 8$$
$$84257 = 9$$

This is much easier to memorize of course, but not as good because you couldn't repeat it at all. If you did, it would become too obvious. I did want to teach it to you so that you could use whichever you like.

Now, there's a way of working this out by simply working the formula backwards, and eliminating all memory work. With a little nudge from my friend Sam Schwartz (who I can never stump with anything mathematical—not for long, anyway)—I came up with the following:—

In order to do it quickly, I take advantage of every possible shortcut for applying the formula. Look; say a *four* is selected by the spectator as the apex card of the pyramid.

Now you want to put down the bottom row which will build to the 4-spot. Okay; place a 3, 6 or 9 in center position. Any of these three cards, in center position, represents *zero*, as I've already explained.

For the two next-to-last cards, use any two cards that *total* nine; an 8 and 1, 7 and 2, 6 and 3, or 5 and 4. This too, represents zero. Now all you have to do is put down two end cards that total 4. A 3 and 1 or 2 and 2 does it. So—if you put down a 3, 2, 6, 7, 1 — it would build to an apex of 4. Work it out and see!

2, 1, 3, 8, 2 — or, 4, 5, 9, 4, 9 — or, 3, 6, 9, 3, 1, etc. — would also build to 4. The only problem with this is that someone who figures out the regular pyramid, *could* figure this, too. The thing to do is make it less obvious.

Let me take it a step at a time. First of all, instead of putting down two end cards that simply total the apex card (let's keep using *four* as the example)—put down two cards that will total 4 *after* the 9s are cast out. For example, an 8 and 5 or 7 and 6. So— 8, 2, 6, 7, 5 — or — 7, 8, 3, 1, 6, etc. — would also build to an apex of 4.

All right; you can cover up further—that is, throw off anyone who is familiar with the '9' principle—by *not* using two next-to-last cards that total 9. For example, use two cards that total, say, 11. You would know, of course, that that breaks down to 2, and then multiplying by 4, gives you — 8.

So—the two *end* cards would have to total a number which when added to this 8—would total 4. For instance, a 2 and 3. (8 + 5 = 13 = 4.) So—a 2, 6, 9, 5, 3 — or — 1, 8, 6, 3, 4 — or — 9, 7, 3, 4, 5 —and so on, would all build to an apex of 4. I suggest you go over these combinations and make sure you understand them.

You realize that I can't give you *every* possible example. Also, I'm using 4 as the example all the way through, but the same ideas apply to *any* apex number from 1 to 9.

You don't *have* to use a 3, 6 or 9 as the center card either, so long as you know that, for example, if you use a number that's *one* higher than any of these (4, 7 or 1)—you'll be working with 6. If you use a number that's two higher (5, 8 or 2)—you'll be left with 3. (No card placed in the center will ever leave you with anything *but* a zero, 3 or 6.)

Okay then; if you want to build to an apex of 4, and you don't want to use a 3, 6 or 9 as the center card, you can use a 4, 7 or ace at center. You're then working with 6. The other four cards must total 7 ($7 + 6 = 13 = 4$). So, you can use, say, an ace and a 7 as the two next-to-last cards. ($1 + 7 = 8 \times 4 = 32 = 5$.) The two end cards must now total 2. So, any two that total 11 would do it.

Therefore—8, 1, 4, 7, 3 — or — 6, 2, 7, 6, 5 — or — 7, 5, 1, 3, 4, etc.—would all reach an apex of 4. Do you see how you can camouflage all this so that it would be virtually impossible for anyone to figure it out? Of course, you'll have to keep at it a while until you're familiar with it.

Finally, if you've followed me so far, you can put down *any* four cards and then simply use the formula to determine the fifth card! Look—still assuming the spectator has selected a 4-spot as the apex—put down any four cards. Say they are a 6, 4, 7, ace.

All right; the 7-spot will be the center card. $7 \times 6 = 42 = 6$. The 4 and 1 (ace) will be the two next-to-last cards; so $4 + 1 = 5$; $5 \times 4 = 20 = 2$. Adding this 2 to the 6 you're carrying, leaves you with 8. You now add this 8 to the 6-spot at the left end of the row—getting 14, or 5. The card you place at the right end must, when added to this 5, total down to 4. You would place an 8-spot there. ($8 + 5 = 13 = 4$.) 6, 4, 7, 1, 8 will reach an apex of 4.

If the first four cards happened to be a 4, 5, 7, 2—the fifth card would have to be another 2 to reach an apex of 4. Do you see why?

Lately I've been using this last idea of mine with this presentation:—I let the spectator shuffle the (36) cards and place *any* five face down on the table. I tell him to turn one face up at apex position. Then he mixes the remaining four, places them in a horizontal row and turns them face up. Now I ask him at *which end* of the row he wants me to place the fifth card. (This doesn't matter of course; I calculate accordingly. It just makes it *look* more difficult.)

As a final example; if the apex card is a 4 and the four cards are an 8, 1, 6, 3—and if the spectator wanted the fifth card at the *right* end (the 6-spot would end up as center then)—my calculations tell me that the four cards total 6. So, a 7-spot at the right end (8, 1, 6, 3, 7) would do it.

If he wanted the fifth card at the *left* end (the *ace* would be center then)—the four cards total 2. So, a deuce at the left end (2, 8, 1, 6, 3) does it.

Well, there you have a variety of ways of doing my 'kicker.' Although I originally always used the 'memory' method, I've leaned more toward the last-described mathematical method, lately. Always camouflaging it, of course.

A final thought or two on presentation:—You can use a deck of number cards instead of regular cards, if you like. Although I, personally, prefer to do it as an impromptu stunt with a borrowed deck.

You can *force* the apex card when you're doing the 'kicker' and leave it face down until the pyramid is built up to it.

Or—pursuing that thought—this could be made to look even more miraculous with *marked* cards!! (Although, to repeat, I like to keep it impromptu.)

Well, you're on your own!!

(Author's note:—In Figure #56, I show the first three cards of the second row of the pyramid above, but not touching, the cards in the first row. This is for explanation purposes. In actual practice, I place the cards in overlapping position, as in Figures 58 and 59.)

OUT OF THIS WORLD MEMORY

IN MY book, *My Favorite Card Tricks*, I taught two pseudo memory stunts. I mentioned then that I use quite a few others, whenever I want to give my mind a rest, and that I didn't want to disclose them. Well, I've mentioned this one at some of my magic lectures, and I thought I might as well mention it here.

In *Close-Up Card Magic*, I taught 'Out Of This Universe,' and the reaction to it has been very gratifying. I constantly hear and read of magicians performing it all over the world.

Again, in *My Favorite Card Tricks*, I taught 'Impromptu Out Of This World.' I mentioned in both books that I rarely used Paul Curry's Out Of This World because, unfortunately, too many laymen knew it. If I do use it, I do the impromptu version as described in *My Favorite Card Tricks*.

I have often, however, used Paul Curry's original version, with a twist or two, as a close-up *memory stunt*. I use it when I'm in a situation where my audience doesn't know that I'm a card man, and when I'm doing only memory (my business) — and I want to give my mind a rest. I've found that it's always accepted as a pure memory demonstration, and causes much comment.

Assuming you know the Paul Curry method, I'll explain exactly how I present this. Have the deck set as necessary, except that fourth from the top, have a card of the *other* color, say—a red card. Memorize the two cards at the center, where the colors meet, one black card and one red card. That's *all* you memorize.

False shuffle the deck and say, "I'd like to try a very difficult feat of memory. I'm going to try to memorize the way the *colors,* not the cards themselves, are lying in this shuffled deck!"

Here you spread the cards faces toward yourself, running through them quickly. And act as if you're trying to memorize the colors by mumbling, "Let's see, two reds, three blacks, three reds," etc., once or twice. (This is when I actually memorize the two center cards.)

Now hand the face down deck to the spectator. "The toughest part of this is that I have to reverse all the colors in my mind. You see, I memorized them from the bottom up—now I want to see if I know them from the top down." (I have to say something like this, since it's obvious that I *have* looked at the cards from face to rear.)

"First, I want one card of each color face up on the table, as leader cards. Let's see, I know the top card is black. Would you place it here, face up? Now, the second, no—the third card, is red. Please put that here." (This is the original fourth card; the one of opposite color.)

Have him place the leaders as you would ordinarily place them. Now you have him place the cards just as usual, except *you* tell him whether they're red or black! Remember, you *must* act as if you're concentrating and trying to remember the order of the colors.

Count the cards as they're dealt, so that you know when to stop and place new leaders onto the dealt cards in reverse order. The two cards you've remembered are now on top of the cards in your spectator's hands.

Again, acting accordingly, say, "I want to make this even more difficult for myself by reversing the red and black cards. So, let me think—yes, the top card is a black one; as a matter of fact, it's the —of—(name the black card you've memorized)." Have him place that onto the 'red' pile.

"The next card, I think, is the —of—(name the red card you've memorized). Anyway, I know it's a red one." Have him place that onto the 'black' pile.

And don't think that off-handedly naming these two cards won't impress your audience no end—*if* you're carrying this off seriously, as pure memory!

And incidentally, you can, of course, memorize the third or fourth, or whatever, red card. I do it the easy way, as described, simply memorizing the two center ones. You can do this any way you like, to fit your own presentation.

All right; now finish with the remaining cards as usual. (Of course, you *don't* have him shuffle these cards!) Be sure to carry through the 'trying to remember' act. I always purposely make a mistake at least once, so I can pick up the card, flash it, and place it on the 'correct' pile, saying something like, "Oh oh, wait a minute, that's my mistake, I think this is red, not black. Hope that's the only mistake I've made. At least I caught that one," and so on. This is a convincer; don't omit it.

When all the cards have been dealt, finish as usual, using the patter line that you hope you've memorized the colors correctly, and so forth. If you're interested in how I end (righting the 'wrong' pile), I suggest you check 'Impromptu Out Of This World' in *My Favorite Card Tricks*.

When you display all the colors in the right places, you've proven(?) that you really *did* memorize all the colors!

Afterthoughts:— Well, that's about it. I don't think it's necessary for me to remind you not to do any 'finger flinging' during this routine. As I've told you, when I do this, it's usually for audiences who have no idea that I know magic—it's done strictly and only as a memory feat.

Be careful during the false shuffling at the beginning, so that you don't lose that one card of the opposite color near the top. Of course, if you like, you can omit this placing of the opposite color card. Simply say, at that point, that the fourth (or any number) from the *bottom* is a red card. Be careful though—the tendency of the spectator may be to turn the deck face up to count to it. You must not allow this, of course. I like to do it as described in the text. And—don't try to memorize that card and name it. This would only make the spectator *expect* you to know others—and would ruin the effect of naming the two center cards, later.

Most important, and I can't stress this strongly enough, you must act this out, all the way through; without overacting. This routine has come in quite handy for me. Perhaps it will for you, too.

DOUBLE BILLEMMA

Here's a routine that has what any good routine should have;
interest, humor and mystery. And—it *isn't* a card effect!

There's a little preparation involved, but you may find it
worth the trouble. You'll need two dollar bills in medium condition
—not too new and not too old. They must have serial numbers in
sequence. That is—the numbers are the same except for the last
digit.

Now prepare the bills so that the serial numbers are the same,
in any of the standard ways. I assume you know how to do this.
You can erase the last digit of the number (in both places) on the
two bills with any good pencil eraser. Do it carefully and neatly,
of course.

Or, if you get the two bills, one ending with an 8 and the other
with a 3—you can change that 3 into an 8 with ink. Done neatly,
this passes pretty close inspection. (Or, if you like, you can simply
remember the last three digits of the number on the bill you're
going to end with; then during the routine, at the point where I tell
you to let the spectator record the serial number of the half bill,
just tell him to remember the last three digits, as you (mis-) call
them. This is easier, but not anywhere as strong as preparing the
bills.)

All right; you have two bills with identical serial numbers. Tear
one of the bills in half; not *too* neatly. You'll need only one of these
halves, so just save the other half. (I used to get very technical here,
and use the half bill that had the tear on the correct side according
to which hand it was in during the routine, and so on. But I found
it made absolutely no difference; so I use either half bill.) You now
have a whole bill and a half bill, each with the same serial number.

Crumple each one into a loose ball. You'll know which is which
because the half bill is somewhat smaller and lighter. Keep them in
an easily accessible pocket.

While doing table magic, you have to load the *whole* prepared
(crumpled) bill into a spectator's pocket, or any place else you want
to produce it from when the time comes. (Your own pocket; a
coffee cup; under a plate, or napkin, etc.)

I prefer the spectator's pocket, and it's not difficult to load it
during a previous trick. When you want to perform the effect, seat
yourself at the table opposite your spectator, and secretly get the
crumpled, prepared half bill onto your lap. Borrow a bill in similar

condition to the ones you've prepared. (It's better to borrow the bill, but you *can* use one of your own, if you don't allow the serial number to be seen.)

Pull up your sleeves, show your hands empty, and pretend to tear the borrowed bill in half. If you don't know this:— Hold the bill up between your thumbs and forefingers, as in (Fig. 60). The left hand turns slightly inward, the left forefinger and thumb slide downward causing the left half of the bill to fold into the right palm. (See Fig. 61). The right hand remains stationary.

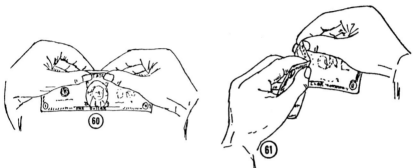

As the fingers move downward, the forefinger nail scrapes against the bill (the bill is between the left thumb tip and forefinger tip, at this point) making a sound quite similar to the sound of a bill tearing. As soon as the left fingers leave the bill, both hands close as if they each held half a bill. Both hands make movements as if crumpling half bills. The sound of the bill *being* crumpled in the right hand seems to come from both hands.

Do this tearing move in one snappy motion and immediately do the crumpling bit. Done correctly, this is a perfect illusion of a bill being torn in half. (For years, I've done this by making the tearing sound with my mouth. A sharp "fffft" does it. This is better for me; use the method that's better for you.)

To continue: Now comes a very important bit of acting. Slap both hands down near the table edge as if you were putting down the two halves of the bill. Say, "Oops, sorry," as you simultaneously lift the right hand, exposing the crumpled bill—*and* acting as if the half bill in your left hand rolled off the table into your lap, nonchalantly reach into your lap, bringing up the crumpled half that's been there all along!

This is the kind of stuff I like to do. It takes no work, just some acting. Do this nonchalantly (I usually look at the floor first, then at my lap, and say, "Oh, here it is") as if you *really* dropped that

left-hand half bill (don't *over*act)—then place it on the table, next
to the borrowed crumpled bill.

I'm partial, of course, but this entire thing, the showing of the
two half bills immediately after the pretended tearing, etc., creates
a perfect illusion of a bill simply being torn in half—if done correctly, of course.

All right; the crumpled borrowed bill is on your right, and the
crumpled prepared half bill is on your left. The spectators, of
course, think they're looking at two halves of the borrowed bill.

Tell the spectator to point to either half bill and using the 'take
it or leave it' magician's choice, get him to select the prepared half
bill. Tell him to open it and to record the serial number. The fact
that he actually sees a half bill here, is the strong point.

After the number is recorded, take this opened half with the left
hand; at the same time, your right hand picks up the crumpled bill
with the fingers toward the spectators and the thumb at the back
of the ball. (See Fig. 62). Slide the bill back toward the edge of
the table, lift it and place it on the open half bill.

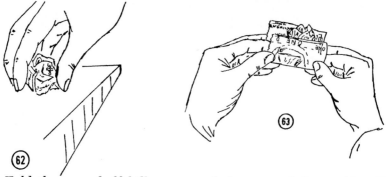

Fold the open half bill up around the crumpled one (See Fig.
63). Start to hand this to the spectator, and accidentally(?) allow
the half bill to fall open, and of course, the crumpled bill falls to
the table.

This is the 'feint.' Now, do exactly the same thing, but when
the right fingers slide the crumpled bill toward the table edge,
allow it to fall into your lap! Do not hesitate for a second. Because
of the position of the fingers, it will appear as if you are still holding the bill. Apparently place it in the open half bill as before. As
you start to hand it to the spectator, again allow the half bill to
fall open, and of course, the crumpled half(?) bill has vanished.

The patter during this is to the effect that you want him to hold
the two halves so that you can't do any 'monkey business,' etc.

Okay; act surprised for a moment at the vanish of the half bill, and then produce the previously loaded prepared bill from the spectator's pocket (or wherever you planted it).

Place this on the table near you and re-crumple the half bill. Say that you will now cause the two half bills to come together by magic. At this point, do any move that makes the spectator think that one of the balls is going into the left hand whereas it actually remains in the right. The left hand remains closed as if it were holding the paper ball. Now the right hand picks up the other ball. Both are really in the right hand.

Make crumbling motions with both hands; slowly open the left, showing it empty. Open the right hand, allow both crumpled bills to roll onto the table, saying, "There, I made them come together by magic!" This is said tongue-in-cheek, of course.

Now say that you will *really* do it. Hold the *half* bill at the left fingertips and the *whole* bill at the right fingertips. (See Fig. 64). Bring the left hand to the mouth, blowing on the bill. The right

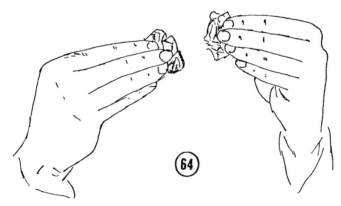

(64)

hand rests on the table edge as this is done. Now bring the right hand to the mouth, blowing on that bill. The left hand moves down to rest on the table edge. As you blow on the right-hand bill, allow the crumpled half bill in the left hand to drop into your lap!

Now bring the hands together as if you were pressing the two crumpled bills into each other. Spread the hands and show that there is now only *one* crumpled ball.

If the moves are done exactly as described above, and almost in beat, in one blend of motion, you'll find that the misdirection is perfect for the vanish of the left-hand half bill.

To end—allow the spectator to open the crumpled bill. He finds it completely restored! Make sure that he checks the serial number against the one he recorded from the half bill. They match, of course.

If you don't want the spectator to keep the prepared bill, you can take it from him under the pretense that you didn't mean to crumple it; and give him a new bill in exchange. You could switch the bill magically—perhaps make it change to two half dollars, etc.

The crumpled half bill and the original borrowed bill are still on your lap. Get them into your pocket at your earliest convenience.

Afterthoughts:— This took some explaining, but is actually a pretty short routine.

Practice the 'bill tear,' the bringing up of the half bill *from* the lap, the lapping of the borrowed bill, and the lapping of the half bill—and you'll have a pretty good piece of table magic.

THE INDICATOR

T HIS IS another almost impossible-to-describe effect. But most every magician who has seen me do it has asked me to write it up. Many different situations can face you during its performance and it would be impossible for me to tell you what to do in every one of these situations.

The basic effect is that four cards are culled and set up for a spelling ending—all during one spread-through of the deck. At the end, it appears as if the four of a kind came up by pure magic. I will again describe this exactly as I do it, spreading from my right hand to my left. You can transpose right and left if you like. If you do, be sure to be consistent and transpose all the way down the line.

Have a deck thoroughly shuffled. Take it and hold it faces toward you. Start spreading, looking for either of the following two situations:— Any pair (two of a kind) with one indifferent card between the two, or, any pair with *two* indifferent cards between the two.

If you do this effect often enough, you'll be surprised at how often you'll find such a pair either at the face of the deck or 1, 2, or 3 cards from the face. If so, you can go right into the routine. If not, keep looking until you find such a situation. There will usually be *several* such situations in any shuffled deck. Try it and see for yourself.

If, and this is quite unlikely, you can't find such a set-up, you *will* find a pair together. Simply slip an indifferent card between the two cards of the pair. Anyway, acting as if you're checking to see if the deck is thoroughly shuffled, find such a situation and cut it to the face of the deck.

Now, shuffle the deck, retaining that set-up at the bottom, and say, "I don't want you to think I've done anything; I just wanted to see whether the deck was thoroughly shuffled. I'll shuffle some more and then I won't change a single card."

I suggest you follow me from here with deck in hand. Let's assume that you have, at the face of the deck, the 5D, indifferent card, and the 5C, in that order. (I'll tell you what to do when there are *two* indifferent cards between the two of a kind, or if there are a few cards *in front* of them—after I've explained the basics.)

All right; I start spreading the cards, faces toward me, from right to left, pattering, "I have to find an indicator card for you. There's usually only *one* particular card that will serve for any particular person. I'll know it when I see the one that fits you. . . ."

As I talk, this is exactly what I do:— I start to spell (to myself), f-i-v-e *on* the *second* five of the pair (I spell the value of whatever pair I happen to be working with). In this example, I start spelling 'five' with the 5C.

When I reach the last letter—the 'e,' I take all those cards (six, in this case) squared, in my left hand (remember, I'm spreading from right to left) and I continue spreading *onto them*. (See Fig. 65).

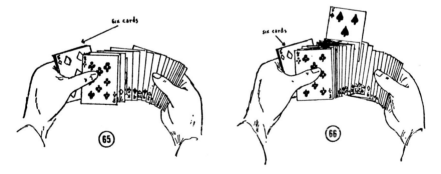

I spread quickly, looking for another 5-spot. When I reach it, I step it up, saying, "Now this may be the indicator card for you; but let me make sure before I make a final choice." I leave this 5-spot stepped up, and continue spreading. (See Fig. 66).

I look for the last 5-spot. As soon as I come to it, I step it *down* slightly, and start to spell its *suit* (to myself) on the card itself. Say it's the 5H. I step it down, spelling 'h.' I continue spreading and spelling, a card for a letter, e-a-r-t-s.

After the 's,' my right hand, carrying all the *unspread* cards, takes the stepped-up 5-spot (See Fig. 67) and places it *face down* in front of the spectator, saying, "Oh well, I'll stick to my first choice. This is the indicator card for you."

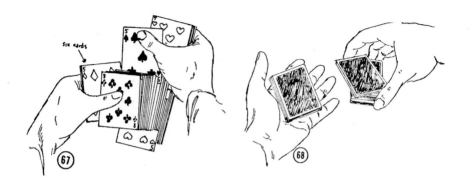

Now I place all the right-hand cards onto the *face* of the left-hand cards and turn the deck face down. The 5H will be injogged at the rear.

Let me pause for a moment to tell you that my patter covers all this easily. Though it has taken a bit of explaining—in actual practice, it takes no more than a few seconds. Follow my instructions exactly, and at this point, you'll have the 5S (in this example) face down in front of the spectator and the other three fives *all set* for the ending. The 5H is jogged at the rear, ready to force.

Yes, you have to force this jogged card and keep all the cards above it intact. There are many ways of doing this. (See Afterthoughts.) Of course, the indicator card must be utilized, otherwise the entire act of searching for it would be senseless.

You can use the standard card-stab force, or—do it as I do:— I push the jogged card flush, securing a little finger break beneath it. Now I double-cut to the break, bringing this vital packet to the bottom and I secure a left little finger break *above* this packet. (I'm assuming you know the double-cut. If not, see "1-2-3 Aces.") And—you'll find that it's a simple matter to secure the break above the vital packet as you square the deck, after the double-cut.

Now I hold the deck from above in my right hand, retaining the break with my right thumb. I tell the spectator to pick up his indicator card and to hold it face down. (I don't want him to see it.)

I will cut small packets into my left hand, and he's to place the indicator onto these left-hand cards, leaving it protruding, whenever he likes.

My right forefinger tip starts breaking small packets at the front end and kicking them into my left hand. (See Fig. 68). When he places the indicator card onto the left-hand cards—I make sure it's protruding outward and I place the right-hand cards onto it for just long enough to leave all the cards below the thumb break on it—and cut the remaining cards to the bottom. (See Fig. 69) to see the action just as I'm cutting the remaining cards to the bottom.

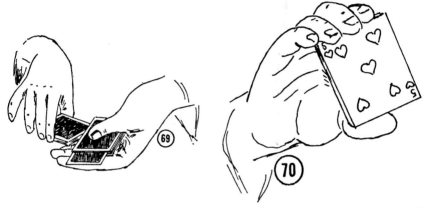

I say something like, "All right, if that's where you want it. . . ." I lift all the cards, up to the indicator card, from above, right fingers at one end, thumb at the other. My left hand deals the indicator card, face down, in front of him, as I say, "We don't need this any longer."

My right hand tilts up so that he can see the card at the face of the packet (See Fig. 70), and I ask him to remember it.

I can't explain this any better. It's quite similar to the Hindu Shuffle force, except that here I'm taking the packets sideways instead of the long way. And, incidentally, the standard Hindu Shuffle force will do just as well if you change it to fit. Suffice it to say that it must look as if he's really had a free choice, and the vital packet is left in your hand at the end. (I realize, as you probably do, that this force is basically illogical—however, perhaps because the spectators believe that the deck is shuffled, it does fool them. It works well for me.)

Anyway, replace the packet to the top and jog shuffle a couple of times without disturbing it. Here's how I end:— "This is really a coincidence effect, and although few people know it, the only

language cards understand, is spelling. Now, if I wanted to spell
your card, I'd spell the value first, then the word, 'of,' and then the
suit. I want to spell your card. What was the value, was it a 3, a 7,
a king—what was it?"

He'll answer, "five." I spell, card for letter, face down in a pile,
f-i-v-e. I turn up the card on the 'e,' saying, "Now, if this *was* a five,
that *might* be just a coincidence."

Leave this five face up on the spelled packet. "Now I have to
spell, of." Start a new packet, spelling, o-f. Turn up the card on
the 'f'—"And if this 'f' were another five, you *know* it's a coincidence."

Say, "Now I have to spell the suit of your card; what was it?"
He'll answer, "hearts." Start a third packet, spelling (do all the
spelling aloud), h-e-a-r-t-s. "And if this 's' *is* your card (it *will* be)
—we're getting into the realm of magic!"

Pause here momentarily, because your audience will think the
effect is over, anyway. Now reach over to the indicator card and
say, "And if this indicator card happens to be the fourth five (turn
it face up here)—then we've seen a miracle!" (See Fig. 71).

71

Well, there you have it. I have fooled everyone (including
knowledgeable card men) with this, and this is the first time I'm
divulging it. Yes—some practice is necessary to get it working
smoothly and without your thinking being obvious.

Now; let's take care of some of those situations that may face
you. First of all, if you start with two cards (instead of one) between the two of a kind, all you have to do is turn the *next* card
when you spell 'of' at the end. That's all. It will work out right,
automatically.

What if, when you look at the face of the shuffled deck, originally—you see, say, three indifferent cards *then* two of a kind with
a card or two between? Remember, the idea is not to change anything if possible, and to go right into the routine. Well, you needn't
change anything here.

Do exactly as described until you reach the fourth card and you're ready to spell the suit. Let's say it's the 5H, as in the original example. If there were *three* indifferent cards in front of the pair originally, your mind works like this: Spell a letter for each of those cards (h-e-a), *then* step down the 5H, continuing the spell. That is, spell the 'r' on the 5H, then t-s, and continue exactly as described. It will work out right, automatically.

Had there been *two* cards in front of your pair originally, you'd spell h-e, then step down the five, continuing the spell, a-r-t-s. In other words, whenever you do this with indifferent cards in front of the pair originally, you *always* (no matter which suit you're spelling) give each of the indifferent cards one letter of the suit *before* you step down the vital card and continue the spell. I'd suggest that you never have more than four indifferent cards in front of the pair (unless you see the club suit in the original pair; then you have a leeway of five indifferent cards).

Here's another possible, but improbable, situation: Say you're working with fives, and as you spell the original f-i-v-e, the third five appears on the, say, 'v.' No problem; simply step it up, as described, but don't consider it in the spelling. Then continue spelling, v-e. When that small original packet goes into the left hand, this stepped-up five just goes along with it. When it's removed later, as the indicator card, everything works out right.

Finally, say you're looking for that last five (5H) and you don't come to it until, say, fourth from the end (top) of the deck. In other words, you step it down, spelling, 'h,' then continue, e-a-r, and you run out of cards. What do you do?

This will be difficult to explain, though it's quite easy to do. I've come to the 'r' and no cards left. I grasp all the cards (except that original small packet) in my right hand. I'm already almost in position. I just put my right thumb on the face card; and hold. (See Fig. 72). My left thumb (which is resting on the face card, anyway) takes cards, singly, from the face of these right-hand cards *onto* the face of the original small packet (See Fig. 73), spelling t-s (or whatever I need). That's all. (To make it clear, picture it this way: any cards you're short for this last spell must be placed onto the face of the original small packet from the face of the deck proper.)

In this instance, it's easier to use my left hand to remove the stepped-up card as the indicator. Then I replace the small original packet to the rear of the right-hand cards, and I'm all set.

Doing this is still logical, since in all cases, what you're supposedly doing is searching for an indicator card. Act that way throughout, and you're safe.

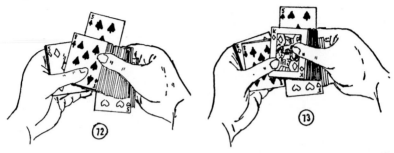

I haven't taken the space to tell you *why* doing what I'm telling you to do in these circumstances will make it work out right. I think that as you work with this, you'll understand it better and *know* why.

Afterthoughts:— Well, admittedly, this has been difficult for me to get onto paper. But after reading it over, I think that if you follow it exactly, you'll get it. Remember that I've described it spreading from my right to left hand; you'll have to transpose if you spread the other way.

Be sure to act (don't overact) as if you're looking for a particular indicator card, as you spread. The correct attitude can cover a multitude of sins.

Here are two other suggestions for the forcing of the vital card, and keeping that packet intact. You can have the spectator hold the indicator card as you riffle the outer ends upward with the right fingers—requesting him to tell you when to stop. Time it so that you're near the break when he stops you, then simply lift off at the break and have him put the indicator card, protruding, onto the left-hand cards. Replace the right-hand packet, pattering for a second, then continue as in the text.

Or—using the hand holding the deck only, drop a packet from the bottom onto the table, to your left; then drop up to the break, to your right; and then the vital packet in the center. Now have the spectator hold the indicator card and either point to, or touch, packets—as you do any 'take it or leave it' force. After the force, be sure to assemble the deck with the vital packet on top.

Remember to do a jog shuffle or two after the force no matter which one you use. I always use the one I've described in the text, but I thought I'd give you a couple of choices.

When you step down the final (fourth) card, it isn't necessary to try to hide it, although it's easy enough to cover. It's logical to simply say, "I could use *this* one, perhaps," as you step it down, and keep going.

It really doesn't matter, since the spectator has no idea what you're doing anyway. And, it happens too quickly for him to get any ideas. I assure you that I can do the entire thing in about 6 to 10 seconds or less—that is, from the time I start spreading until I put down the indicator card. There's no need to appear hurried, however.

At the beginning, stress the fact that the deck is being thoroughly shuffled since, to magicians anyway, this is not particularly difficult to duplicate using a *set-up* deck. Of course, it wouldn't be much of a trick that way. It's the shuffling at the start that makes this strong.

When I originally spread to find a pair, I don't look too long. If I don't find the situation I want, say, within 13 to 16 cards, I'll either hand the deck back to the spectator asking him to give it another shuffle or I'll shuffle myself. The odds are that now I will find a pair quickly.

I'm kind of proud of the way this routine is put together, so please practice it until you really can do it well.

I know that I say this quite often, but I feel it's important: get this to the point where you can do it without hesitation and *without your thinking showing*, and you've got a miracle on your hands!

OH, THOSE ACES!

A NOTHER tongue-in-cheek presentation idea I tried on some other magicians originally, and found that it fooled them completely. Perhaps this is so because I lulled them with what looked like an old idea, and then, too late, they realized they'd been 'had.'

The effect is that the shuffled deck is cut many times and cards are moved haphazardly from packet to packet. Finally, four packets are cut by the spectator, and an ace is found to be the top card of each.

There really isn't much to this; basically, I think, it's your acting ability that's most important. You're sitting at a table opposite your spectator and you've lapped the four aces.

I'm not going to go into a long explanation on lapping the aces. I get them to the top during a previous trick, then palm them off and leave them on my lap, or under my thigh. The important thing is to do this at the right time so that it isn't seen, and *not* to go into the routine *as soon as* you've lapped the aces.

I've mentioned this before (in other books), I know, but it still needs mentioning, obviously, because I still see some magicians get a key card ready, or lap cards, and then immediately go into the trick which utilizes that key or those lapped cards. That's usually wrong, unless you're particularly adept at spotting and setting key cards and lapping cards.

And—although I guess I can do these things as well as anybody, I still like to use what I call, 'time misdirection.' After I've lapped the aces, I *always* do at least one effect first which has nothing to do with the aces; *then* I do the effect for which I've lapped them.

All right; tell the spectator to cut the shuffled face down deck into two halves. Then to cut each half in half again. He has four face down packets in a row, in front of him. As you talk, let your hands be seen to be empty, without calling attention to that fact.

Point to the first packet; tell him to pick it up and to take the three top cards and place them to the bottom. Now he deals one card at a time, from the top of this packet onto each of the other three packets. He replaces this packet.

Now have him pick up the second packet and repeat exactly. That is, duck three cards then deal a card, apiece onto the other packets. Have him do this with all four packets.

This, of course, is the old idea I mentioned. I'm sure you know it—if you start with the aces on top, they'll end up one on each packet, etc., etc.

This is what lulls other magicians into complacency. What I usually do is have him duck *four* cards (instead of three) one time. The psychology (and it's the psychology that fools other magicians) behind this is that they think, "Well, he's added a new little twist somewhere, but it's still the same old thing."

When he's done the same with each packet, have the spectator re-assemble the deck, placing one packet on top of the other, and so on. But—point to packets, giving him instructions as if it's important as to which packet goes onto which. It *is* important to keep your hands near the cards, acting helpful. This is to help camouflage the 'move,' later on.

At this point, another magician should sit up and take notice.

Because, if you *were* doing the old idea, the aces would be lost now. Have the spectator cut the deck into packets again, and move top cards from one to the other, haphazardly. Re-assemble again and give the deck a complete cut.

I've asked magicians to whom I've shown this and they told me that about here they started to think that I was kidding them. That I was just making them work and that I had no ending. They became lulled again, and did what I asked just to be polite.

You have to judge just how long to drag this out. I go just about as far as I've described. Now—have your spectator cut the deck into four packets again. As he's doing this, palm the four aces into your right hand. Only the right hand should go under the table top; the left hand keeps helping with the instructions.

When he's formed the four packets, have him move a card or two from one packet to another and then point to the first packet on your left with your left hand and tell him to place this onto the packet *at the other end.* This is because I want him to make the longest move possible here.

At the moment he's moving this packet, you pick up the packet now at your left of the row, with your right hand, adding the palmed aces, and place it onto the adjacent packet to the right— in the same movement. (See Fig. 74).

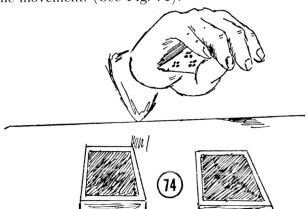

This *must* be done nonchalantly—you're merely helping him to assemble the packets, and you can even make a remark to that effect, as you do it. Immediately point to the half deck *you've* just assembled and have him place it onto the other half. The aces are on top.

Have him cut the deck into four packets again. Now *don't* do that old idea of ducking three cards, etc. Have him move a card

at a time, in a seemingly haphazard order, from packet to packet.
(He's accustomed to this by now.) Make it haphazard looking,
but manage to get the aces, one on top of each packet.

All that's necessary here, is for you not to make it obvious that
the three top cards of the one packet are going onto the others.

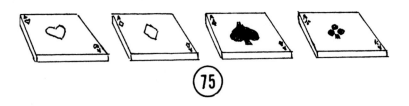

(75)

Keep moving them around so that the spectator is confused. (Be
careful not to confuse yourself.)

To end—turn up each top card to display the four aces. (See
Fig. 75).

Afterthoughts:— Need I say more? Be sure to lap the aces im-
perceptibly and use 'time misdirection' as I discussed. Add the
palmed aces at just the right moment, nonchalantly, and you'll
'knock him on his ear.'

I must admit that the old idea of having the aces on top and
doing the three-card duck with each of four packets, etc., can be
just as effective to most laymen—if the deck appears to be fairly
shuffled at the start.

But—since I, personally, don't really like this type of trick—if
I do it at all, I want it to look like more of a 'miracle.' I would only
do it this way (as I've just taught) for laymen, particularly per-
ceptive ones. And—I get a kick out of fooling other magicians.

You don't necessarily have to use the four aces, of course. The
date of a coin or bill which you've noticed (or switched), and so
on—is just as effective.

TEN CARD POKER DEAL

A LTHOUGH this is *not* an original idea—the routing is mine.
I don't know how far back the basic idea goes. The first
reference to it that I could find was in Arthur Buckley's book,

Card Control; in which he devoted only *one* short paragraph to the idea, treating it as a puzzle.

I believe that Dai Vernon once had it in the magic magazine, The Phoenix, titled, The Mexican Gambler, or Mexican Poker, or something similar. I know he included it in his book, *Inner Secrets Of Card Magic.* And Bruce Elliott discussed it in his book, *The Best In Magic.*

Well, now it's my turn! So far as I know, the idea has never been definitely *routined* and I don't think that its *entertainment* value has ever really been stressed or demonstrated.

I'm writing this because at every magic lecture I do, when I let the magicians make requests as to what they'd like me to perform and teach—this is always requested. Whenever I perform it, I'm asked for the routine and to explain the little touches I've added through the years.

The entertainment value is limitless. Many times, I've had large groups of people practically in hysterics with it. They're laughing at the impossibility of it and at the spectator who is trying to beat me—but in a good-natured way. In other words, no one is ever embarrassed by it. Everyone gets involved, because they're 'kibbitzing' and trying to help the guy playing against me.

I use the following ten cards: 5C, 5S, 5H (or 5D), AC, AH, AD, KC, KS, KH (or KD), and the QC. I *always* use these ten cards. That way, I don't have to think about which cards I'll use when I'm starting the routine; and I become familiar with all the combinations and possibilities. (See Fig. 76).

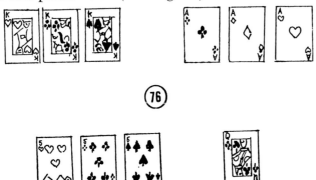

(76)

The odd card, the Queen of Clubs, is the key to the whole thing, because whoever gets it in his hand *must* lose. I want to hide this card as much as possible. That's the reason I use two black and one red five and two black and one red king, not the other way around. And, of course, I don't use the Ace of Spades because it's too conspicuous.

You might think that using two black and one red jack instead of the fives would camouflage the QC even more. It doesn't work that way. It tends to pinpoint it, and aside from that, it would make it too confusing from the visual angle. Suffice it to say that after many years of experience with this, I *always* use the ten cards listed above.

Now for the routine, from beginning to end. I'll comment on the reason for certain things as I get to them.

Ask if there's one among your spectators who plays or knows poker. Have him sit opposite you at the table. Patter: "Many times, after having done some of the miracles (tongue in cheek) that I've done for you here, I'm asked if I can win at poker even if someone else does the dealing. My answer is that it doesn't matter *who* deals—I'll always win if I want to. And I'll prove that to you right now."

As you get into this opening patter, start spreading through the deck, locating the ten cards. Either step them up in the spread or place them face down on the table, as you come to them. Don't let the spectators see the faces; there's the possibility that someone will try to remember the cards. As you do this, tell your audience that you're looking for ten special cards. Once or twice, as you find one, say, "Yes, I think this is a good one," or, "I think I'll use this one," etc.

Have the QC either on top or bottom of the packet of ten cards. Locate, and leave the AS on top of the deck proper as you find and remove these ten cards. This is for a reason that I'll explain when the time comes. Place the deck off to your right and hold the ten-card packet in your hands.

Patter: "You and I are going to play head-to-head poker with just these ten cards. Let me tell you why. Many people ask me about palming a card. I don't know what that is—I think it means trying to hide a card in your hand something like this." Here I hold a card in my hand in almost palm position, but sloppily, awkwardly, and with half the card visible. It gets a laugh. Replace the card.

"But even if I *could* palm cards, if we play with only these ten, it wouldn't do me any good. When we dealt out the two hands, it would be obvious that we were one card short. If I surreptitiously *added* a card by palming, you'd know it too, because we'd have

one card too many. Okay? Now, you've only been taking my word
for the fact that there are exactly ten cards here. Let me show you
that there *are* exactly ten."

Here I count the cards by dealing them face down slowly and
obviously from a height, so that they fall to the table. I do it with
one hand, and I count out loud. I keep track of the QC as to
whether it's on top or bottom.

"Now, no matter who deals, I'll always beat you." As you talk,
shuffle the packet, getting (or keeping) the queen on top. I use
jog shuffles only. This is a bit awkward with only ten cards, and
I *say* so occasionally as I shuffle. So long as it looks as if the cards
are being mixed.

"For example, this is just a demonstration. I'll shuffle them as
well as I can shuffle such a small packet and I'll deal them out
straight." Suit action to words, and deal the two hands. He, of
course, gets the queen as his first card, and can't win.

"Now pick up your cards and see what you have. As a matter
of fact, lay them down so everyone else can see them." I always
pick up my hand, holding it fanned, and I don't let anyone see
my cards.

When he puts down his hand, say what he has out loud. Then
take *only* the cards from your hand that beat his hand and lay them
face up on the table so everyone sees them.

For example, if he has, say, a pair of kings, you'd have two pair,
aces and fives. *Show the aces only.* If he had, say, three fives, you'd
have a full house with either three kings or three aces top. Show
only the three of a kind, *not* the full house. The reason for this is
that it creates a bit of mystery, and more important, your audience
will rarely see all ten cards at one time. (See Fig. 77). I show my
entire hand only when I *have* to. I don't allow the cards to remain

face up very long, in any case.

"All right; I won that hand, but of course, *I* dealt. Now I want you to see that it really doesn't matter who deals." As you talk, pick up the cards so that the QC is *second* from the top.

Now this is used throughout the routine, so it must be done neatly. I can't explain exactly what to do, since it's according to how he lays down his cards. If the queen is already second, simply pick up his five cards and drop them face down onto yours. If it's on top (bottom really, since the cards are face up), use another card as a scoop. If it's third, fourth or fifth, take as many as necessary from the rear of his cards (See Fig. 78), drop them onto the face, then drop your cards, which are being held in your hands, face up, onto his—and so forth.

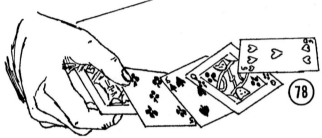

Learn to do it neatly, nonchalantly, and without hesitation. Even though you're going to shuffle the packet, any hesitation or nervousness here, will signal the fact that you're doing (or arranging) *something*. Patter as you pick up and don't act suspicious. (Of course, you can pick up the cards as they lie, noting the position of the queen—and then run cards during the shuffle, until it's in position.)

All right; jog shuffle, keeping the queen second from top. Hand the packet to the spectator, saying, "Here, I know what I'll do. Start dealing the cards straight."

As soon as he's dealt one to you and one to himself, say, "Now stop. We'll do something that's never been done before. I'll let you shuffle the stock before you deal another round. In non-technical terms, that means you can shuffle those eight cards before you deal another card apiece. Go ahead, shuffle them. Now deal another card to me and one to yourself."

Let him do as you instruct. Then say, "Now shuffle again; now deal another card apiece. Keep doing that, and I'll still beat you!" When he has only two cards left, say, "You can mix those two, if you like, before you deal them out. I'll beat you anyway."

Let him deal the last two cards. "Okay; see what you have and lay the cards on the table. You have three fives? Oh, oh, I think you've got me now. No, you gave *me* three kings! I don't think you understand; I *want* you to win. Here, let's try it again."

I use that line, "I *want* you to win," as a running gag, as you'll see. At this point, and this is the only time, I pick up so that the queen is *third* from the top.

I spread the cards face down in my hands, in front of him. "Here, just touch any card. That one? Okay, take it." What I do here, is try to force the third card from the top—the queen. Although I try to force it the first time, it doesn't matter, since I have five chances. As soon as he takes the queen, I lay the remaining cards, face down and spread, onto the table, and say, "Let's see, you've got one; here, take the other four yourself—and I'll still beat you!"

If he takes the queen on the second draw, I do the same thing, changing the patter accordingly. The object is to lay the cards you're holding onto the table as soon as possible. On the rare occasion that you can't seem to force the queen on the spectator you're working with, turn to another spectator, saying, "Here, help him out, you take a card for him," and force the queen on *him*. Have him place the card with the others that have been selected for the spectator's hand.

If the top or second card is selected first, I always shuffle and add an indifferent card onto the top. This is only because I feel it's easier to force the third card than the second. And please, never use anything but the standard classic force; any other force would look silly here. It's *got* to look as if he simply selected *any* five cards.

He has five cards in front of him. "All right, I've let you take your own hand, and I'll still beat you. Let's see what you've got."

Whatever he's got, show that you've beaten him (always name your hand), and say, "I don't understand you—I *want* you to win! Here, let's try it this way——"

Pick up the cards—QC second from the top. Shuffle and hand him the cards, "I know how to really make you win. Start dealing out the hands." Let him deal only one card apiece. "Now stop. Let's pretend that these cards are marked. Of course, they aren't, so I'll let you look at each card, like this." Reach over and lift up the top card so he can see it, but you can't. Replace it to the top.

"Now you know that top card, right? Who do you want to give it to—yourself or to me?" Let him deal it to whomever he likes. "All right; now look at the next card. Who do you want to give that one to? In other words, I'm going to let you look at each card. You can give it to whomever you like; even if you take three in a row, or give me three in a row; as long as we end up with five apiece. I'll leave it entirely up to you. The only thing I ask is that you deal the last two cards straight, without looking."

This last remark is meaningless. It doesn't matter at all how he deals the last two cards. I just say it to confuse the issue; it's a 'red herring,' is what it is. And—later on, it helps it appear as if I'm giving him an extra.'edge.'

Let him look at each top card (one at a time) and deal it as he likes. He can't win, no matter what he does. You make comments according to how he deals. For example, if he has four cards already dealt to himself and you have only two, you might say, "Now you already have four cards; if you take one more, you have to give me the rest, so be careful." If he does take his fifth card and still has cards left, say, "You want that one? All right, but now you have to give me the rest," and so on.

If he gets down to only two cards, say, "All right, I told you that you'd have to deal the last two straight and without looking. Well, I'll give you a break. Go ahead, look at the top card and give it to whomever you want."

When he's through, say, "Okay, let's see what you gave yourself. Two pair, aces and kings? Well, I just don't understand you! You gave *me* three fives! No, you don't seem to understand, I *want* you to win!" (If you don't have the people laughing heartily by now, you're doing something wrong!)

Pick up the cards, QC going to second from top. Jog shuffle, as you say, "I think I know what the problem is. It's a memory problem. You're having trouble remembering which cards you've already dealt to whom. Well, I'll solve that for you. Up to now we've been playing closed poker; let's play stud, or open, poker. Here, take the cards and deal out just the two hole cards."

Let him do so. Then stop him and pick up your card; let him see it, but you don't look at it. "Now, I'll put you 50% ahead of the game by letting you see my hole card. I don't want you to see yours yet—but now you know mine. So, go ahead; look at each card, one at a time, and deal it to whomever you like. But remember, we're playing open poker, so deal them face up so we can all see them. Now you'll have no memory problem; and no excuses, either."

Let him deal; you make appropriate remarks as he goes along. Just as in the preceding deal, remind him that he can take or give two or three at a time, but also let him know when he can deal only one more, or two more, to a hand, etc.

When he looks at the second card he's to deal, I usually say, "And, if you're not too sure who you want to give a card to—why, put it back and shuffle so that you'll get another card to the top. I don't want you to strain yourself making decisions!"

This always gets a laugh (because he usually *is* undecided) and also makes the routine stronger. Make sure he shuffles when he puts back a card. I never let him put it to the bottom, or second from top, because I don't want him memorizing the positions of cards.

When he deals me a five, I usually say, "Sure—thanks a lot!" If he deals me an ace, or—if he gives me a card which would have given *him* a pair—I usually look at someone else in the audience and say, "You know, he's the first one who ever did *that*. I think I bit off more than I can chew this time." (You should say this during this particular deal just once, in any case.)

You have to rely on 'feel' here. It's difficult for me to tell you *exactly* what I say and *exactly* when I say it. There's so much room for gags and laughs, I'm sure you'll know and 'feel' just what to do and say. The lines I'm writing here are basically the ones I use.

When he's finished dealing, turn up your hole card and call your hand. (This is the only time you show your complete hand first. If you let him show his first, the QC would remain exposed longer than necessary.) He turns up his hole card and of course, you've won. Pick up the cards, with the QC either on top or bottom this time, as you say something like, "I don't know what else I can do with you—you just don't want to win, do you?"

Now at this point, I usually do the ending I'll explain in a moment. But you have a choice here. I don't use this too often, because usually, the routine is just long enough as it is, with the ending. When I feel I want to prolong it, I'll use this. Or, more often, I'll just use *this* as the end (if I use it at all).

Remember that AS you left on top of the deck? (When I'm pretty sure I'm going to use this, and if circumstances permit, I sometimes *lap* the Ace of Spades at the very beginning. Then it's there if I need it.)

Well, you can hand the ten cards to the spectator and have him shuffle. Palm the AS as you toy with the deck. Tell the spectator to deal the cards out straight and you'll still beat him.

What you do is—as he deals each card to you, look at it, leaving it on the table, which is a natural poker-playing action. If you don't get the QC, simply lap the AS—and you've beaten him. Build up the fact that he shuffled and that you never touched the cards, etc. (You *could* corner crimp the queen so that you don't have to look; but I *never* do.)

If you *do* get the queen, and as soon as you get it, add the AS to the hand. The ace can go anywhere, but be sure the queen is on top. Now you can turn your hand face up and spread it, keeping the last card (the queen) hidden behind the fifth card.

But—and this is a big 'but'—this will *not* always be the winning hand! I never sat down to *really* check this, but I believe there are four hands he can get that will beat yours, even with the AS. For example, either full house consisting of aces and kings will beat you. Two pair consisting of two aces and two kings will beat you, because you'd have two aces and two fives. Three aces will also beat you—and I think those are the only four.

So, you're taking a chance. The thing is this, there's a 50-50 chance that you won't get the queen. And most (about 7 to 9, I guess) hands dealt (with the queen) will win for you with the AS. So the *odds* are, you'll beat him.

Just so I've impressed upon you that this *is* chancy. And there isn't much of an 'out' either. First of all, you'd have to *know* that you have a losing hand *before* you expose it. This is simple enough, once you're familiar with the hands.

I have some outs, but I really don't think they're worth the space I'd have to take to explain them. (This is taking more space to explain than I thought it would, as is.) I'm sure you can work out your own if you want to.

I *do* use this occasionally, as I've said. I don't mind taking chances and I can get out of it if I have to. If you feel you can, fine. Otherwise I'd suggest you forget about it. It isn't necessary to the routine at all.

The only reason I've included it is because so many magicians have seen me do it that if I left it out, I'd be accused of holding something back! (And—it's good to know about in case you ever *need* it for some reason.)

I'll leave it to you whether you want to use this or not.

Now then, to the ending I always use. You've just finished the open poker deal. Shuffle the ten cards, getting the queen to the bottom. I always use what I call the 'slip-shuffle' to keep it there. This is an overhand shuffle while applying light pressure with your left fingers and thumb. This leaves the top and bottom cards in the left hand during the first move of the shuffle (See Fig. 79)—and the remaining cards are shuffled onto these. Now drop the ten-card packet onto the deck proper.

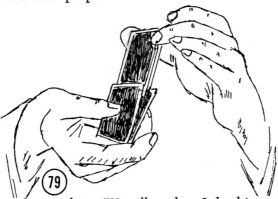

The patter during this:—"Usually, when I do this, someone asks, 'What if we use the entire deck?' Well, it makes no difference, and I'll prove it to you. Here (as if you just thought of it) give them a good mixing." (Don't say, "the ten cards," here—say, "them.")

At the last sentence, pick up the deck and take *nine cards only* from the top, handing them to the spectator. Now this *must* be done nonchalantly. It doesn't matter if the audience sees you counting, since you're supposedly counting off the ten cards. But—don't count them one at a time, because someone may count along with you!

I always spread and *sight* four cards and then five cards, or vice versa. Or, you can do it by sighting three, three and three. Whichever you use, do it smoothly and quickly without appearing rushed. The key is *nonchalance*.

As soon as you hand him the packet, place the deck onto the table near him and say, "Now put the cards on top." This doesn't give him too much time to shuffle (or think).

Let me assure you that during the thousands of times (literally) that I've done this (for laymen and magicians), it has *never* been questioned, nor has it aroused any suspicions whatsoever.

All right; now say, "Okay, you've shuffled the ten cards, and I haven't touched them, and I *won't* touch them. Please pick up the deck and deal the two hands off the top, straight out."

He does so and of course, he gets the queen! During the dealing, keep your hands obviously away from the cards. Don't go near your hand either. This is too good and too strong to ruin by making your audience think you've 'done something.'

Don't let him look at his cards. The two hands are left on the table. Patter: "Now, you've shuffled the cards thoroughly and I haven't gone anywhere near them. So you *know* that *one* of these hands must be the winner. There's an even 50-50 chance for each of us. Right? Right!

"Let me ask you a question. If I were to bet my *million dollars* against your dime that *I* have the winning hand, would you take the bet? And, remember, I won't touch anything. Would you bet your dime against my million bucks?"

If he answers, "yes," say, "Then you're a lousy gambler! You should know better than to bet against a 'pro.' You've just lost a dime; go ahead, see for yourself!"

If his answer is, "no," you say practically the same thing, "Then you're a smart gambler! You've learned something here. You know better than to bet against a pro. Because I've got you beat; go ahead, see for yourself!"

Let him turn over the hands and see that what you say is so. Then pick up the ten cards and *shuffle them into the deck.* And that's it!

Afterthoughts:—I don't think you can appreciate the entertainment value of this routine (unless you've seen me perform it for laymen) until you try it. Practice, and learn it until you understand it thoroughly, and *feel at ease* with it. Presentation is of utmost importance here.

It's the *entertainment* value I'm after. Without that, this is nothing but a puzzle. This routine makes it entertaining, a fooler, and something your audiences won't forget. You'll get plenty of credit for being a great card handler and take my word for it—you'll be asked to do it again and again. (Be careful of repeating it for the same people, however.)

If a spectator ever asks if he can shuffle *before* he deals the first two cards, simply say, "Don't worry, I'll do better than that"—and keep going.

And please—and I've said this before—don't start changing it too much. Of course, you may want to change the patter to fit you, but don't change the routine. Rely on my experience, and I've had plenty with this.

One final and important point; don't *ever* use a 'wise guy' or 'see how clever I am' attitude with this. Laugh along *with* (not *at*) the spectator, always.

Here's the routine in steps:—

1. Take out the 5C, 5S, 5H (or 5D), AC, AH, AD, KC, KS, KH (or KD), and the QC.
2. You shuffle, you deal—as a demonstration.
3. He deals a card apiece, then shuffles; then another card apiece and shuffles, etc.
4. Force the queen (3rd from top) and then let him take remaining cards himself.
5. He deals a card apiece, then looks at each card before dealing.
6. Open poker; he deals hole cards, then continues as in Step 5, but face up.
7. He shuffles *nine* cards, then places on deck. Deals straight.
8. You glow with satisfaction as your audience carries you off on their shoulders!

(Publisher's note:—I have seen Harry *fracture* a roomful of people with this. I don't think there could *possibly* be a stronger, more entertaining routine with cards than this—not as Harry presents it, anyway.

So, although you may have already known the 'secret' of the odd card, I think you'll agree that Harry Lorayne has again contributed a 'classic' to card magic, by routining this to the 'nth' degree.

It is no longer a puzzle; it's a classic 'reputation-making' routine! Study it; learn it—and you've more than received your money's worth.)

COINTROL

H ERE'S a quick coin routine that I've used for years. It's done while standing; and is all based on sleeving. The sleeving moves I use are not original with me and they really can't be described in print. It's the routine that makes this a good, magical quickie. I must assume that you know the moves, although I'll try to describe them as well as I can.

The way it looks to the spectator:—You borrow a penny and display it on the left palm. You make a gesture with the right hand as the left hand closes. Open the left hand to show that the penny has changed to a quarter.

The quarter is replaced into the left hand. The left fingers squeeze and then open to show that the quarter has vanished. Both hands are shown empty. The quarter is produced from your trouser crease. Now the quarter is visibly changed back to a penny as it falls from hand to hand.

Method and presentation:—Reach into your pocket with the right hand, palming a quarter and openly bringing out a penny. You can borrow the penny if you like. Place the penny on the open left palm, and do the sleeving move which sends the penny into the right sleeve, and leaves the quarter in the left hand. (I don't know who originated this sleight, but the late Emil Jarrow used it for years.)

Basically, the penny on the left palm is propelled into the right sleeve *as* the right-hand coin is dropped into the left hand. (See Fig. 80).

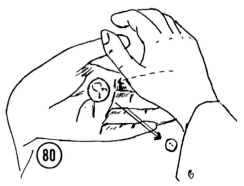

This is the part which just can't be explained or described in print. Assuming you know the sleight, I can only give you a few tips. Most important, the left hand shouldn't appear to move at all; it is held stiffly, palm up. Actually, it has to move only the slightest bit in order to propel the coin into the right sleeve.

Also, with practice, it should appear as if the right hand never gets too close to the left hand. The entire movement of the right hand should look like a magical gesture. The larger movement of the right hand covers the very slight movement of the left hand. The left hand immediately closes on the quarter. (This is a beautiful sleight if done properly.)

Squeeze the left fist; gesture with the right hand, showing it empty, and say, "If I squeeze the penny, instead of getting smaller, it gets larger and looks like a quarter." Open the left hand; take the quarter with the right fingers and display it.

Now do the 'pumpkin seed' vanish as you apparently place the quarter back into the left hand. This sends it into the left sleeve.

Succinctly, this is the move in which the coin is held with the right thumb and forefinger at its *edge*. (See Fig. 81). As the left hand approaches to take it, the left hand turns palm down apparently taking the coin. The right fingers apply pressure, squirting the coin into the left sleeve. (See Fig. 82). Of course, you act as if the quarter is in the left hand as the left fist is turned palm (or fingers) up, immediately.

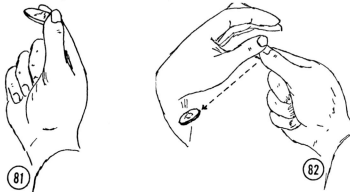

Again gesture with the right hand, showing it empty. Squeeze hard with the left fist, saying, "This time, if I squeeze real hard, the quarter gets so small, you can hardly see it!" Open the left hand; the coin has vanished.

Say, "I know; you're wondering where it went. Well, here it is right in the crease of my trousers." As you talk, lower both hands to your sides. Both coins are delivered, one into each hand. Palm the penny in the right hand as the left hand produces the quarter from the trouser crease. You can, of course, produce the quarter from wherever you like. It's most natural for me as described, since it is just a continuation of the downward movement of the left arm.

Display the quarter on the open palm of the left hand. I usually turn it once or twice with my right fingers, as I talk. Patter: "Of course, you know I started with a penny; well, that's true, and if I simply toss the quarter through the air, you'll see that the air changes it back to its original form, a penny!"

This final move is the same as the first move of the routine, but I've embellished it a bit to make it look different and even more magical. As you gesture magically over the exposed quarter, it is sent into the right sleeve and the penny is deposited on the left palm, as usual. In this case, the left fingers do *not* close. The left hand (in a continuation of its original slight movement) moves upward; the right hand turns palm up, and the left hand tosses (tilts and pushes) the penny so that it falls down into the right palm. (See Fig. 83).

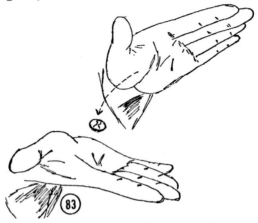

All this must be done in one fluid action. If done smoothly and properly, it looks as if the quarter actually changes to the penny in mid-air, as it is falling. This will take some practice and eventually, you'll get it. Until then, you can do the regular move, showing the coin changing on the left palm.

Afterthoughts:—I usually borrow the penny. At the end, I do a coin roll with it and return it to the spectator.

I don't like to keep my right arm bent, waiting for an opportunity to retrieve the quarter. So, sort of as an afterthought, and as I say, "Oops, I don't want to let that quarter get away"—I reach up with my left hand as if to grab a quarter from the air. At the same time, I drop my right arm to my side. This delivers the quarter into my right hand.

Now both hands approach each other and I pretend to place the 'caught' quarter onto my right palm. Time this properly, exposing the quarter just as you pretend to place it on the palm, etc., and it looks like what you want it to look like.

This entire routine must be done in one blend of action from start to finish; and at a pretty snappy pace. Practice it; make it 'flow,' and you'll want to use it often.

THE ROYAL LOVERS

THIS IDEA belongs to Sid R. Spocane II. He graciously gave me his permission to write it up for this book. The handling is his, except that he uses the king and queen of diamonds to magically find the four aces. I use the four jacks instead; they fit the patter theme better.

There is a slight set-up necessary, but it needn't be done previously. The KD and QD are removed from the deck and the jacks have to be set up on top in this order: JD face down on top, then any other jack face down, then the remaining two jacks *face up*.

You can do this easily while attention is elsewhere and you're toying with the deck. Or, as I usually do it:—As I look for and remove the king and queen of diamonds, I get the four jacks to the top, making sure the JD is uppermost.

I ask for a spectator who thinks he's sexy. There's room for laughs here. I ask him to examine the KD and QD, which I have face up on the deck. As I spread the top cards in order to remove these two, I manage to spread four face down cards. I throw the KD and QD to the table and square the deck, securing a left little finger break beneath the four jacks.

As he picks up the two diamond cards, I lift the two top cards from above, with my right hand, as if I were going to do a double-lift.

I remove these two cards together and place the inner left corner into the break. (See Fig. 84). Now, with the left thumb acting as the fulcrum, I use these two cards to flip over the other two. (See Fig. 85). In the same motion, I drop the right-hand cards onto the reversed cards.

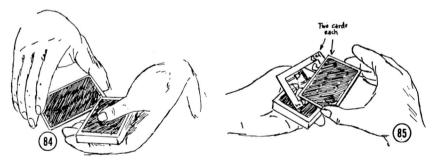

Done correctly, in one fluid action, this is almost instantaneous. It's easy enough to do it as your spectator examines the KD and QD. Start it the moment he looks down at them as he goes to pick them up.

That's how I set up. Now for the routine. Patter to the effect that the queen was not very faithful to the king; she had many lovers. The king was suspicious of course, but the queen was very clever about it.

As you talk, obtain a left little finger break beneath the top card of the deck. Take the king and queen from the spectator with your right hand. Place them face up onto the deck as if to square them. *Do* square them—*with* the top card, the JD.

The right hand lifts the three cards from above and the left thumb immediately slides off the face card. (See Fig. 86). The figure shows the face card in the process of being slid off and onto the deck.

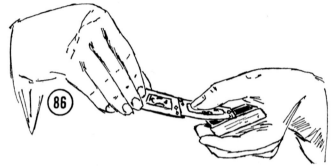

Now place the right-hand card(s) onto the card you just slid onto the deck. (See Fig. 87). Square the cards (really three; spectators think there are two) and hold them at opposite diagonal corners as in (Fig. 88).

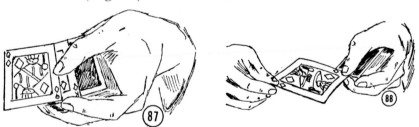

Tell the spectator that you want him to hold the two cards this way and to gently move his hands up and down. All this is hardly essential, of course. Basically, it's an excuse for taking the two cards into your hands in the first place, and for handing them back to the spectator.

Have him hold the cards and gently move his hands up and down. What I mean here is—he alternately moves his hands in opposite directions; one upward and one downward, causing the cards to bend slightly, almost as if the cards were being crimped.

When he does this, say, "Mmm, you *are* sexy; you do that beautifully." Or, something to that effect. This is up to you; you can make it as strong as you like.

Tell him to spread the two cards; a face down card appears between them. He turns it up, displaying the JD. Say, "See how cleverly the queen got her lover into the castle?"

The only reason for having the JD on top is to have it appear first. It makes more sense, since you're using the QD and KD. If this doesn't matter to you, however, you can set the jacks, at the beginning, in *any* order.

All right; while he was doing the 'sexy' moving of the cards, etc., you have secured a left little finger break under the top *three* cards of the deck.

What has to be done now, is this:—You place the king and queen *face up* on top of the deck, and then turn over *all* the cards (5) up to and including the break. Then you have to lift off the three top cards, as two.

To avoid the thumb-counting after the turnover, and to make it look neater, do it this way: *Still maintaining the break,* place the KD and QD face up, and flush, onto the deck. Now pull the top face card back toward you about half an inch.

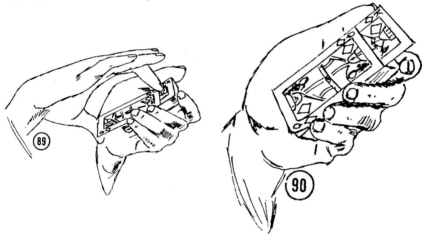

Place your right thumb at the inner end of this card and your right second fingertip onto the face of the second exposed card. (See Fig. 89). Now push outward gently. The inner end of the deck acts as a 'stop' for the right thumb tip, as the two cards move forward.

The situation is: The top face card is flush with the deck; the second face card is out-jogged about half an inch. (See Fig. 90). This is all done openly, as you say something like, "Now watch the king and queen."

The right thumb and first and second fingertips pick up all the cards up to the break, at the inner right corner. (See Fig. 91); and turns them over (face down) *outward,* onto the deck. This means that the card that was out-jogged it now *in*-jogged. (See Fig. 92).

The right thumb pushes in and *down* on this jogged card which almost automatically leaves (or delivers) the cards (3) above it in your right fingers. (See Fig. 93). Immediately start sliding off the top card with the left thumb, and do the exact same actions as before, when the king and queen were face up.

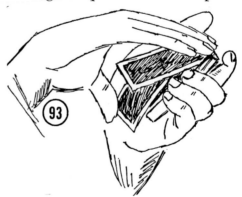

Hand him the cards, face down this time, and have him do his 'sexy' movement. Tell him to spread the KD and QD, and there's another 'lover' face up between them.

Don't let him turn over the two face down cards. These are the other two jacks, and you don't want to kill the climax. You take the face up jack from him, and drop it onto the table with the first one.

The trick of course, is all done, as far as you're concerned. Here's how I usually end:—Put the deck down and take the two face down cards from him. Square them and do that 'sexy' movement. Then hand them back to him, in squared condition, and have him do the 'movement.' When you hand the cards to him, say, "Here, you take the king and queen and do that movement you do so well." What you say is immaterial, so long as you mention the king and queen.

Now tell him to spread the king and queen apart. Act surprised when no third card appears between them. Milk this for a moment and then tell him to turn the king and queen face up. Your last line of patter could be, "Well, you really *are* sexy, aren't you? You don't care about the king and queen at all; you're just interested in the lovers!"

The deck is clean and the trick is over.

Afterthoughts:—If you don't mind doing a thumb-count lift-off of the three cards after you've done the five-card turnover, you don't have to worry about the out-jog, in-jog business I described. I *do* use it, however.

Done correctly, it's fast and neat, and practically *delivers* the right cards into your hand, at the right time. It should appear as if you're doing it just to display the king and queen. It eliminates the thumb-count, which has to be done while your audience is looking at your hands. (Of course, there are other ways of avoiding the thumb-count.)

The king and queen are face down on top of the deck at the end and you can palm them off or reverse them, or what have you. I don't bother. The ending is strong enough as is. I just put the jacks back into the deck and shuffle; that's all.

You don't have to use the patter theme I've suggested at all. You can use *any* two cards to find any four cards. For example; ask the spectator to name any pair of reds or blacks. Say he names the black eights. Search through the deck for the eights, getting the four aces to the top at the same time.

The patter here could be that you're lucky he named the black eights, because they're the only two cards with which this trick will work, etc. Meanwhile, get set up.

Then use the eights to magically find the aces. This is a good lead-in to other four-ace routines.

FARO BLOCKBUSTER

I DON'T imagine that too many of you will use this routine. I think you'll be missing out on a good thing if you don't use it. The basic effect is that three red cards and three black cards are used to prove that 'oil and water' don't mix.

Then, after showing that the deck is well mixed, these six cards are placed, separated and reversed, into it. The deck is (faro) shuffled three times, and when it is ribbon spread (face down), there are three face up pairs consisting of a red and black card each. Now the deck is turned face up and *all* the reds and blacks are separated!

First of all, you have to be able to do a perfect faro shuffle. And, almost the entire deck has to be set up as to reds and blacks. I do this right under the spectators' noses, and I suggest you do the same. I'll try to explain exactly how I set up the deck, and how I do the routine. It's going to take a bit of space, as you'll see; but I believe it's necessary. Now, if you're willing to work a little; here goes:—

I usually set up *half* the deck (or more) during a preceding trick as I supposedly look for a selected card. I explained this idea in detail in "Out Of This Universe" in *Close-Up Card Magic*. (I suggest you check it.) For completion's sake, what I do basically is—I either force or control a card. I tell the audience that I can find the card only by elimination.

I spread the cards with faces toward me as I look for the selected card. Acting as if I'm eliminating cards, I set up about half the deck. I get the selected card to the top. I say that I think I've found it, and do a double-lift. Of course, he denies that this is the card. I place this (?) card face down onto the table, and ask for another chance.

I continue looking, setting up some more cards. I either do it *all* here, or *almost* all. I'll explain this in a moment. I end by showing that the tabled card has changed to the selected card.

Now I say that I need six special cards, three red and three black, for another trick I want to perform. Leaving the selected card face up on the table, I look through the deck for five more cards to add to it. This is where I finish the set-up, if necessary.

I think I'd better explain the set-up before going any further. Any three reds and three blacks are used for the effect; that leaves 46 cards to set up. From the face of the deck up, starting with red and *alternating* colors—the set-up is:—3, 3, 3, 4, 3, 2, 3, 2, 3, 4, 3, 3, 2, 3, 3, 2. This means, that from the face of deck up, you set 3 reds, 3 blacks 3 reds, 4 blacks, 3 reds, 2 blacks, etc.

Don't give up! I'll even tell you how to memorize this. Also, in a normally shuffled deck of cards, you'll find that the first 6, 9 or 13 cards of the set-up can be found ready and waiting. What I mean is—if you spread quickly, you may just find 3 reds, 3 blacks, 3 reds in that order, and so on.

So—what I usually do is look for something like this and cut it to the face of the deck. The trick works as well, incidentally, if you start with *black* cards and alternate. I always start with the (3) reds at the face, to avoid confusion.

In "Out Of This World Memory" I taught you how to fake the memorizing of colors, now I have to teach you how to really do it. If you've read *How To Develop A Super-Power Memory*, or any of my other books on memory, you know that certain consonant sounds representing certain digits, is a form of mnemonics. I don't want to give you an entire memory course here, and you don't need it in order to remember the set-up.

In my system, the letter (or sound) 'M' represents 3; 'R' represents 4, and 'N' represents 2. Those are the only digits necessary to memorize this set-up. So, I've always used the nonsense phrase, "*MuM MoRMoN MaN; My RooM MiNiMuM? No.*"

Do you see? Once you know the digits (2, 3 or 4) that the letters (N, M or R) represent—memorizing that nonsense phrase is the same as memorizing the set-up!

Forming a picture in your mind of what this phrase means to *you*, will help you to memorize the phrase itself. You should have all this in mind in no more than a few minutes.

When you're setting the deck, simply repeat the phrase to yourself as you go. Start with reds and always alternate colors. I usually finish. "*MuM MoRMaN MaN,*" which is exactly half the set-up (23 cards), then do the double-lift, etc., as I explained before. Then I continue setting up from there, as I supposedly keep looking for the selection.

There's another mnemonic device to help memorize the set-up. I don't like it or use it, but again, for completion's sake—make up a phrase or sentence (logical or nonsense) containing words in which the *amount of letters* tell you the number. One example:— All(3) the(3) red(3) tape(4) can(3) be(2) cut(3) if(2) the(3) tape (4) has(3) all(3) of(2) its(3) lid(3) on(2)" I repeat, I don't like this method. It can cause confusion as you set the deck. I'd suggest you stick to, "MuM MoRMaN MaN; My RooM MiNiMuM? No." I leave this to you.

Later on, it will be necessary for you to cut the deck (46 cards) exactly in half. As you set the deck, if you note the first card as you start setting the second half (after you've double-lifted), this will act as your key for the cut. This, of course, is the 24th card from the face of the deck.

All right; let's assume then that you've had a card selected and in searching for it, you've set the deck and noted the 24th card from the face. There are six cards on the table, three red and three black.

The patter should pertain to oil and water (or people) not mixing. And do just one or two fast 'oil and water' routines with the six cards. I'm assuming you know some of these; certainly enough methods have been published.

What I use most often, is probably the simplest one. Place the three, say, blacks, face up onto the face down reds. Spread to display this (See Fig. 94), then square, securing a break over the lowermost card.

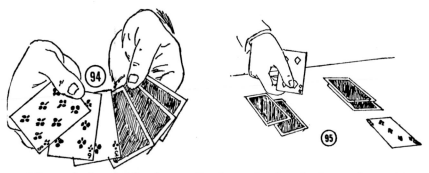

The right hand lifts the cards above the break, from above. Now do the add-on move (see 'Foursome'), saying, "One black, two blacks, three blacks." The first two are flipped face down. The third one (?) is dropped face up onto the packet.

Now deal that face up black card onto the table. Deal the next two cards, face down, beneath it, saying, "Here are the three blacks."

Deal the next two cards, face down, to the left (or right) of the blacks. The last card is turned face up (it will be a red card) and placed above these two. (See Fig. 95). "And here are the three reds."

Switch the two face up cards, saying, "But if I put this red card with the blacks and this black card with the reds, you'll see that they just won't mix." Turn all the cards face up to show that this is so.

This is really a 'follow the leader' effect, but the patter makes it all right, and it serves the purpose.

Here's one more:—This belongs to my good friend, Herb Zarrow, who gave me permission to include it. Spread the six cards face up between your hands, showing, say, the blacks *on* the reds. The left thumb tip rests on the black card (8C) that's furthest to the left. (See Fig. 96).

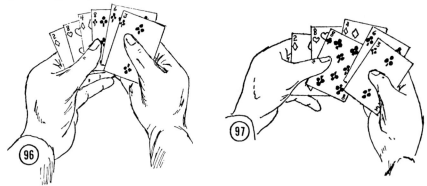

Underneath the spread, the right fingertips rest on the red card (4D) that's furthest to the right. Now—the 'move' appears as if you simply turn the cards face down taking the three reds in your left hand and the three blacks in your right.

As you turn your hands over (toward you) and the cards face down, separate your hands—the left thumb pulling the black card (8C) into the left hand and the right fingers pulling the red card (4D) into the right hand. (See Fig. 97), which shows the move at about mid-way. The two cards simply change places.

The hands continue moving, placing the three-card packets face down onto the table; one to your left and the other to your right. Say that you'll alternate (or mix) the reds and blacks into one packet.

With your left hand, take the top card of the left packet, flash it, saying "red," and place it, face down, between the two packets. The right hand takes the top card of the right packet; do *not* flash it, place it on the center card, saying, "black."

Continue alternating this way onto the center packet, flashing *all* but the next-to-last card. (That's the last of the left packet.) Practice this so that you can do it in beat, without hesitation. It's completely convincing. Now snap your fingers, or what have you, and turn the packet face up to show that the reds and blacks just won't mix.

I've given this a quick description. It deserves better; I just don't have the space. I'd suggest you give it the practice it deserves. Anyway, there you have two ideas for 'oil and water' quickies with the six cards. Use them, or whichever you like—but no more than two or three.

Now—patter, "So you see, reds and blacks won't mix; unfortunately, sometimes people won't mix—but given enough opposition, sometimes strange things happen. Watch, I'll lose these six cards among all the other cards. I'll leave them face up so we can find them easily."

Turn the deck proper face up and do a wide ribbon spread, mentioning that the cards are all mixed. (You can do a false shuffle or cut before you spread, if you like.) The cards, of course, do appear to be in a naturally mixed condition.

Break the spread in half at the card you noted before. This card goes to the face of the top half. Turn both halves face down and remember which is which. (If you can cut the deck exactly in half without a key card, then naturally, you can forget about that.)

Here's what has to be accomplished:—The three red (or black) cards must go into 2nd, 6th and 10th position from the top of the *bottom half*. The three black (or red) cards must go to 3rd, 8th and 12th from the top of the *top half*.

It doesn't matter where the reds and blacks go, as long as the three cards of each color go into the same half. And, of course, it must look as if the cards are being *haphazardly* lost into the deck.

Here's how *I* do it:—I make sure that the six cards are spread (separated) and face up on the table. I pick up the *bottom* half and hold it face down in dealing position in my left hand. I deal *one* card into my right hand. Holding it from above, I place this one card onto one of the face up say, red cards. I slide these (two) onto the half in my left hand.

As I approach the left hand, I start spreading *three* cards with the left thumb. As I drop the two onto the half, I form a break under the three I just spread (that's five cards altogether) and immediately take all these (5) and drop them onto the second face up red card. (See Fig. 98). I slide (or bring) these to the left-hand cards.

As I approach, my left thumb starts pushing off *three* cards again. As I drop the smaller packet onto the half, I again form a break under these three (nine cards above the break now); immediately lift all above the break and drop them onto the third face

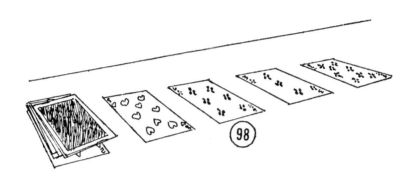

up red card. I bring all these back onto the left-hand cards. Now I do a double-cut, without changing the position of any card. This has placed the three face up reds into 2nd, 6th and 10th position!

This is not easy to describe. Try it with cards in hand as you read, and you'll see what I mean. I keep talking as I do this and it does appear to be a haphazard insertion of the three cards.

Drop the top half deck *onto* the half you've just been working with. Now you're holding the complete deck (except the three blacks) in your left hand. You can do the same thing for the three black cards. This time you'd take *two* cards the first time, then spread and break *four* cards and then *three* cards. This places the three blacks—3rd, 8th and 12th.

Or, what I usually do:—Hold the deck in the left hand with the thumb at the outer left corner, ready to release cards one at a time. The forefinger is bent under the deck. (See Fig. 99). The thumb releases two cards. The right hand inserts one of the face up black cards there. Leave the card protruding. (See Fig. 100).

As you insert this card, the thumb starts releasing four cards. Place the second black card there. As you insert that, start releasing three cards, and place the last black card there.

Push the three cards flush and you're set. Again, I usually do a double-cut here, keeping all the cards intact. So; I usually place the three cards into the bottom half as explained; drop the top half onto it and then use the thumb-count release for the placing of the other three. Or, of course, do the same with the second set of three as for the first, as I said. It's according to how I feel.

The only other suggestion I can make is that you can fan the cards and place the three reds or blacks that way. So long as it looks haphazard and natural. It must *never* look as if you're counting.

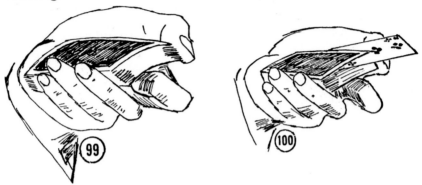

Now—pattering to the effect that you really want to lose the three red and three black cards, do a perfect '*in*' faro shuffle. Meaning—you cut exactly in half and the top and bottom cards are lost during the shuffle; they become second from top and second from bottom respectively.

Incidentally, if you used a key to cut the deck in half prior to the insertion of the six cards, that same key is still at exact center, so you can use it for the cut of this first shuffle. It's cut to the face of the top half. And—you should use a fairly new deck, otherwise the opposite bend of the six reversed cards may make the shuffle difficult.

Do another (second) perfect 'in' shuffle. After this second faro, do a wide *face down* ribbon spread, showing that the six reversed (face up) cards are widely separated throughout the deck. Now square the deck (I usually do a false cut or two at this point) and do one more perfect 'in' faro shuffle.

All the work is done. All that remains is to build up the ending. The patter theme I use is that when placed among all that opposition (the other 46 cards), and after all that shuffling, sometimes the reds and blacks *do* mix.

Do a wide face down ribbon spread to display three face up pairs, each consisting of a red and black, spaced throughout the deck. (See Fig. 101). Take these pairs out of the spread, giving this first climax a moment to register.

I usually say something like: "But unfortunately, in the world we live in today, when lots of people live close to each other, they sometimes still refuse to mix."

Punctuating this last remark, I flip the spread face up in domino fashion (if I'm working on a good surface—otherwise I simply

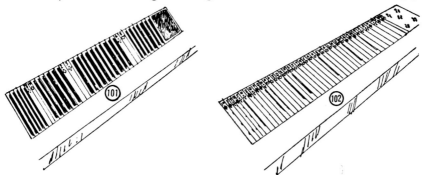

square and then do a face up ribbon spread), showing that all the reds and blacks are separated!!

Afterthoughts:—Well, this should keep you busy for a while. Of course, I could have written it in half the space, but that would have been doing you and the routine an injustice, I think.

I didn't include too much patter because I feel this is up to you. You have to fit the patter to the speed and the manner in which you work.

Also, it can be made as strong and as topical as you like. The civil rights movement, and etc., fits in perfectly.

After the second faro shuffle and after showing the six cards spread throughout the deck, the deck can be given as many straight cuts as you like. It will still work, except that the red (or black) cards will be sandwiched between the black (or red) cards, at the end. (See Fig. 102).

When you place the three cards face up into the bottom half as I taught, don't be too neat and square the cards too well. Let it look sloppy, which helps it appear haphazard.

Memorize the amounts of cards that have to be spread from the top, when you do this. Of course, the six positions should be well memorized, so that you don't have to stop to think when placing these cards.

I told you that I set the deck right under the spectators' noses, and I believe that's the best way to do it. I don't like taking a deck out of my pocket and going right into a routine of this kind. Of course, if you *do* pre-set the deck, be sure to do some false shuffling before you start.

Or better still—memorize the six cards you're going to use, set up the deck—then place one of the six at the bottom and distribute the other five throughout the deck. Now cut the deck a few times. When ready to perform, cut the deck, then do a face up ribbon spread. Push out the six memorized cards as if you're taking just *any* cards. Cut the deck at the spot where you placed one of the six at the bottom, originally—and you're all set.

Well, practice this routine and learn to do it well and you'll have added a 'blockbuster' to your repertoire.

Good luck!

ONE-EYED JACK SANDWICH SEQUEL

WHEN I wrote "One-Eyed Jack Sandwich" in *My Favorite Card Tricks*, I didn't mention this because I thought most magicians would think of it, anyway. So far as I know, nobody did. It's a good four-ace (or any four of a kind) lead-in.

This description will be short because the basic idea is described in detail in *My Favorite Card Tricks*.

The four aces are face up on the table. Pick up the two red ones, leaving them face up and put two face down indifferent cards between them—on top of the deck.

As you display, secure a break beneath the top face up ace. Do a double-cut, bringing this ace to the bottom. No other cards change position. The situation is as in (Fig. 103).

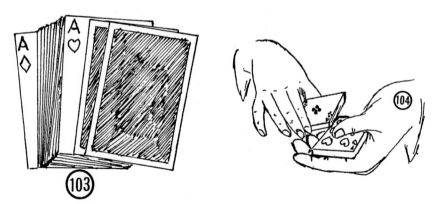

Take the two black aces and place them, face down, to the bottom. Now turn the deck face up.

Patter: "You know that somewhere in the deck are the two face up red aces with two cards face down between them. But you don't know where they are. Neither do I. I don't want you to know where the two black aces are either, so I'll cut them into the deck."

The cut that's done here, as I've said, is described in detail in *My Favorite Card Tricks.* The only difference here, is that you must break *two* cards (instead of one) at the rear of the deck. Here's a quick description.

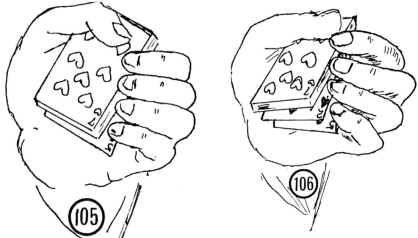

Hold the deck face up in the left hand. The right hand cuts half the deck from above as in (Fig. 104). The left little fingertip pulls down one card at the rear of the left-hand half. (See Fig. 105).

As soon as that's done, the left *third* fingertip pulls down the next card. (See Fig. 106). The width of the breaks are exaggerated in the illustrations, of course.

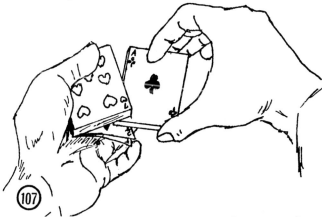

The right-hand cards are placed into the space between the lower half and the two pulled-down cards. (See Fig. 107). And the deck is squared.

Your left side should be slightly toward your spectators as this is done. That way, they can't see anything that looks suspicious.

Of course, you can release the cards that your third and fourth fingertips are holding as soon as the right-hand half enters. You should pause here for a second, then square. Done correctly, it looks *exactly* as it should; a legitimate straight cut.

The work is done. This one move has removed the two indifferent cards from between the red aces and placed the black aces there instead!

Turn the deck face down and spread until you come to the two face up aces with the two face down cards between them. "Here they are. The two indifferent cards between the red aces. But watch."

Take the four cards out of the spread, make your magic pass or gesture, etc., and show that the two black aces are now between the red ones. Your last patter line might be something like, "Well, it seems as if birds of a feather really *do* flock together!"

Afterthoughts:—Nothing more I can tell you about this, except perhaps, when you break the card with your left third fingertip, you can release the one held by the little fingertip.

That way, the third fingertip is holding both cards away from the half deck. This isn't necessary, of course, since these two cards are held for only a fraction of a second, anyway.

This is a good quickie, but I wouldn't use it at the same sitting during which I use the "One-Eyed Jack Sandwich," or vice versa.

I originally described the cut (retaining one rear card) in *Close-Up Card Magic* in an effect called, 'The Spectator Estimates.' At that time, Ed Marlo advised me that this was his move—and that he'd published it. I checked and found this to be true. He called it the 'Pull-Down Move.'

As I said in *Close-Up Card Magic*, I've used this move since I was a child—which is no big deal, since it's the kind of thing that many others might have thought of, or used, simultaneously. (Three other magicians told me that they too have used it and never read it anywhere.)

Anyway, Ed *did* have the first published description of it, so far as I know. I promised to mention this in print the next chance I had. So—I just mentioned it.

MODERNIZED SLOP SHUFFLE

J. BENZAIS, a good friend, and one of the cleverest of the New York magicians, contributed this effect. A card is selected and lost. Then the deck is mixed face up and face down, as in the Slop Shuffle; then the deck is spread to show that all the cards are facing one way, except the selection.

The natural opposite bend of reversed cards does the trick—but if you want to play it safe, you can give the entire deck one sharp downward crimp (or do a pressure fan) before you start. You'll find, however, that the natural bend will be enough—after some practice.

All right; control the selected card to the bottom. Now for the mixing. Hold the deck face down and in dealing position. Spread about ten cards, from the top, into the right hand. Turn this hand over, which turns the cards face up. Spread (about ten, or so, each time) more cards into the right hand (under the thumb) *beneath* the first group. (See Fig. 108).

Turn the right hand over and spread-deal some more cards *onto* its cards (under the thumb). Jog these downward, so the face up cards stay visible. Turn the right hand over, and spread-deal some more *beneath* them (under the thumb).

Turn the right hand over again and spread-deal *all* the remaining cards, *but one, beneath* the right-hand cards. They go under the *fingers* this time. The last card (face down selection) is brought to the top; and the deck is squared.

Follow this exactly as I've described it, and you'll be all right. The easiest way to remember it is:—Aside from the last card (the selection), five packets are spread into the right hand. Each one goes beneath the right thumb, except the last group, which goes beneath the right fingers. And, of course—the right hand turns over before taking each group.

If you've done this correctly,. you'll actually have two face up groups in the face down deck. One directly under the top face down card; the other group—near center. Quickly spread the deck once, between your hands, showing the reversed cards. Now square the deck and follow the handling carefully.

From above, with the right fingers, lift off the small packet up to the natural crimp. Turn the right hand up a bit to show cards back to back. (See Fig. 109).

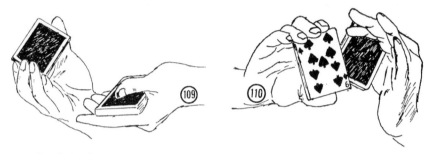

The left thumb flips over the deck proper, bringing a face up card into view. Place the right-hand packet back on top, slightly stepped, to show the contrast of a face up and face down card. Now square.

Flip the entire deck over. Cut to the first natural break (about ten cards from the top), showing cards face to face. Do *not* flip the deck over. But—place the right-hand packet to the bottom and tilt the left hand up, displaying the face up, face down contrast. (See Fig. 110).

The right hand never releases its packet. As the hands turn down again, buckle the bottom card (selection) of the deck proper. The right-hand packet goes into the space thus formed, (See **Fig. 111**)—and square the deck.

Now cut to the next natural break (about ten cards). Show the cards back to back at that point. Flip over the deck proper. Replace the right-hand packet on top in stepped position, displaying the face up, face down contrast. Square the deck, securing a left little finger break above the face down card.

At this moment, this is the *only* face down card in the deck— it's the selected card! End like this: take the deck from above with the right hand; thumb retaining the break.

Undercut some cards from rear to face, so that the break is now at about center. Say, "Here's a face up card," as you do this. The trick is all done now, but as a final convincer:—Undercut *half* the cards up to the break, showing a face up card; then *replace* the packet. Now cut to the break, showing a face down card, and replace this, re-securing the break.

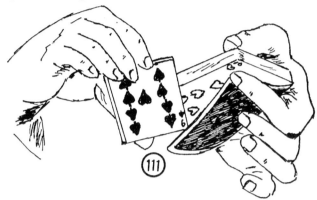

Cut a small packet from the top, showing a face up card. Replace, and cut to the break again—showing a face down card. Replace, without holding the break.

Ask for the name of the chosen card. Do a wide face up ribbon spread, showing all the cards facing one way, except for one face down card, at about center. Turn this up to show the selected card!

Afterthoughts:—It will take a while to get this all set in your mind. Just put in some practice time.

After doing the mixing—the cutting at the end is done quickly and without pausing. You're supposedly cutting at different areas in order to show the deck in a mixed condition. As you cut, say, "Here's a face up card, face down card, face up card," etc.

I've included this effect because I like it and use it. It is, however, more of a magicians' effect than a laymen effect. Although I use it for both. It's just that, for a layman, you can probably get the same effect with the regular slop shuffle—if it's done well.

I, personally, would rather use this modernized version. It's your decision.

MENTAL PHOTOGRAPHY

THIS appeared in Hugard's Magic Monthly magazine some years ago. At the time it appeared, the late Fred Braue said, "This is not only an excellent card feat, but in it you've been given a real prize—the Lorayne Self-Index. 'I've never thought twice about my substitute for the card index,' Lorayne writes, 'because I've used it since I was a child.' You will think more than once about this invaluable idea: it opens up all those feats you may have passed over because of dislike for bulky, bothersome card indexes."

This entails using a blank deck and some preparation. Learn this, and I think you'll find that it's worth it. Here it is just as it originally appeared:—

This is what the spectators remember afterward:

You display a deck of cards with regular backs but with blank faces. You fan the deck, hold it faces toward a spectator and ask him to think of any card except a court card.

Then you square the deck and shuffle meticulously. You explain that you're going to give the spectator certain instructions; he is to follow them, dealing cards onto the table, etc., when told. You demonstrate with a few cards.

You hand the deck to the spectator and turn your back. You instruct him to double the value of his card and to deal that many cards onto the table. Then you have him deal one more card for a club, two for a heart, three for a spade, and four for a diamond.

He drops the deck onto the dealt cards; and cuts. You take the deck and glancing through it, you confess that while you have received an impression of the suit, you are still having trouble with the value of his card.

You hand him the deck, turn your back, and have him repeat the dealing for the value.

The deck is placed into your hand. You have the thought-of card named. You spread the deck face up displaying one card among all the blanks. It is the spectator's mentally selected card!

Method: You'll need a deck of 51 blank-faced cards. You'll also need a pocket card index. If you have one and can use it, fine. If not, do as I've always done. I have the four suits from Ace to ten, each in a different pocket. I use the pockets that I can get into with my right hand. For example; right trouser pocket, right jacket pocket, shirt pocket, and left inside jacket pocket. In this way, I can palm any card directly into my right hand.

I set each suit from ace to ten; ace on the bottom and the ten on top, of the packet. Give each packet a sharp downward end-to-end bend. Take the 6, 7, 8, 9 and 10 and turn them back to back with the lower five cards. In other words, the 5-spot and 10-spot of each suit will be back to back.

The ace will be at the face on one side, the six on the other. The crimp makes it easy to stick the forefinger between the 5 and

10-spot. The most you'll have to count, in any case, will be three cards. (See Fig. 112). You count from the face inward or at the crimp, from back outward, according to the card you need.

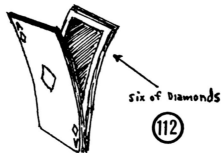

six of Diamonds

(112)

Play with this a while, until you're familiar with it. I've always found it as easy and as fast as a pocket index. Just be sure you know which way each packet faces, and in which pocket you have each suit. Also, be sure you know which way the card is facing after it is palmed, so you can get it into the deck facing the right way.

The entire presentation should have a tongue-in-cheek flavor. You must create the impression that the instructions you give are silly and worthless, and couldn't possibly help you, because all the faces are blank. Try to create the impression that you're making up the instructions as you go along.

When you fan the deck and ask the spectator to think of a card, he may think you're joking, so be sure he understands that you really want him to think of one.

"Think of a card, any card, except a picture card. It's much easier to see a spot card in your mind. I haven't perfected this yet, and I don't want to make it too difficult for myself."

Now, there are quite a few methods for determining the name of the thought-of card. Some of these methods permit the spectator to shuffle and cut whenever he likes. I've found that it really doesn't matter to the spectator whether he shuffles or not, because the cards are blank and he sees no way in which you can know his card, anyway.

In my presentation, however, you'll see that the spectator gets to shuffle and cut at just the right times.

Here's the simplest way of learning the name of the spectator's card. Prepare the blank deck by placing a pencil dot on the face of the top and bottom cards. I usually place the dots at the extreme of two diagonal corners.

To present, take out the deck and shuffle it, keeping top and bottom card intact. Show that the faces are all blank. Now shuffle once more, like this:

Undercut half the deck. Run six cards and injog the next one. Shuffle off, but make sure the bottom card falls last (on top). Form a break at the injog. Run the top card singly, then shuffle to the break. Throw the rest on top.

This has placed one pencil-dotted card to seventh from the top; the other key is still on the bottom.

(Shuffling a blank deck, of course, is an absurdity, but it carries out the "motif" of the trick, and is therefore psychologically useful. If you have trouble with the overhand shuffle, however, you can omit it by placing the dotted cards to seventh from the top and to the bottom, before you begin.)

All right; the spectator thinks of a card, and you say, "This is an experiment in mental photography. I want to see if I can actually get a photo of your thought. But—before I can do that, I have to know what that thought is; in other words, I want to try to read your mind. I can do that only if you concentrate. And I'll help you to concentrate by giving you instructions which you are to follow implicitly."

Tell him to double the value of his card and to deal that number of cards from the top, singly and silently, face down onto the table.

In order to demonstrate, you add, "If your card happens to be a deuce, you would double two and arrive at four. You'd deal four cards onto the table, like this. . . ." Deal four cards singly as you talk, to demonstrate. "Then I may tell you to deal one or two more . . . but let's do that while my back is turned."

As you say, "One or two more," deal two more cards, as if to demonstrate.

"When you're through, you'll drop the deck onto the dealt cards, like this." Demonstrate, explaining that the deck should then be squared.

What you've accomplished here, is to really demonstrate what you want done. Also, you've psychologically shown that the cards are really mixed. You now have a dotted card on top while the other one is seventh from the bottom.

Turn your back, and tell the spectator to go ahead and double the value of his card, and to deal that number of cards, singly and silently, onto the table.

Now tell him to concentrate on the suit of his card. If it is a club, he's to deal one more card; if it's a heart, he's to deal two more cards; if it's a spade, three more, and if it's a diamond—four more.

Now he drops the remainder of the deck onto the dealt cards. You turn to face him as you tell him to cut the cards and complete the cut. Have him cut again. (I always let him cut two times. That way, a key card will end up somewhere near the top or bottom. This is the key on which I start my count in a moment, as you'll see.)

Take the cards and spread them faces toward you. What you have to do is count the cards between the two keys, including the first key card in your count, but *not* the second. Whatever the number you arrive at, deduct *six*. Now you know how many cards he dealt all told.

Your covering patter for the spreading and counting, could be, "If I were doing a standard card trick, I'd just look through all the cards like this, and most likely, find your card. But in this case, looking at blank faces does me no good at all. But do concentrate on your card; that will help me. . . ."

Knowing the number of cards the spectator dealt gives you a choice of two cards, one of which *must* be his mentally selected card. For example; if he dealt 12 cards—any *even* number tells you that the card must be a heart or diamond. (Odd numbers represent black cards.) Twelve cards means he thought of the 4D or the 5H.

You arrive at this quickly: For even numbers simply subtract 2 and 4. (The number of cards moved for hearts and diamonds.) Two from 12 is 10. Divide by two to arrive at 5. One possibility, therefore, is the 5H (because you subtracted 2, for hearts). Subtracting 4 from 12 leaves 8. Divide by 2 to get 4. Second possibility; 4D (because you subtracted 4, for diamonds).

If the number of cards dealt is odd, do the same thing, except you subtract 1 and 3, for clubs and spades. Example: If 7 cards were dealt, you would subtract 1 for clubs and divide by 2. The 3C is one possibility. Subtract 3 for spades and divide by 2; 2S is the second possibility.

Once you get familiar with this, you'll be able to arrive at the two possibilities almost instantly. And if you perform the routine often enough, certain amounts of dealt cards will tell you the possibilities by memory.

All right then; after running through the cards once, you can look at the spectator and say definitely that he's thinking of a red card. (Assuming you found that he dealt 12 cards.) Now say, "I think it was a heart." His yes or no at this point, will tell you which card he's thinking of.

Hand the deck to the spectator. Off-handedly tell him to shuffle. "I know the suit of your card, but I can't seem to get the value. I'll have to ask you to concentrate again. I'll turn my back. Will you double the value of your card and deal that number of cards as you did before? But this time, please concentrate harder as you do it."

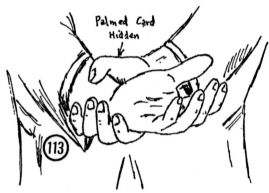

This is all meaningless, since you already know his card. It gives you the excuse to turn your back and get the necessary card palmed into your right hand. Remember to keep your elbows pressed to your sides so that no movement can be seen from behind you. You should have the card palmed before he's through counting, and rush him a bit by asking him if he's done.

Turn to face him and ask if he really concentrated this time. As you talk, put your hands behind your back and grasp your left wrist with your right hand which still holds the card in palm position. When he says he has concentrated, turn your back to him, still holding your left wrist, and holding your left hand palm up and open. (See Fig. 113).

Tell him to place the deck face down in your hand. (This is a good way of hiding a card; it looks completely natural.)

Turn to the front, keeping your hands behind your back. Slip the palmed card into the center of the deck (be sure it goes in facing the right way) quickly, and immediately bring the deck forward.

Have the spectator name, for the first time, the card he's thinking of. When he does, say, "You are the only person in the world who could know that card. Now let me show you the power of your thought."

Do a wide, face up, ribbon spread on the table. There, face up in the center, is the card he just named!!

Afterthoughts:—My original description explained this pretty thoroughly, so I've changed only a few things here and there.

The reason for using a deck of only 51 blank-faced cards is simply that after adding the thought-of card, you're left with 52 cards, in case anyone wants to count them.

I don't think it's necessary for me to tell you that the backs of the blank cards and the backs of the index cards must be the same.

You can do this using the picture cards, of course, It's just that my index idea fits ten cards per pocket much better. And—I find that it makes absolutely no difference to the over-all effect.

When counting the cards between your keys, the count *must start* on the key that was on *top* when the spectator started following your instructions. If you anticipate any confusion as to which is which after his two cuts—simply 'dot' that card a bit differently, so that you'd know one from the other. If you present this exactly as I've explained, the key that you have on top before you start, is the one that is on top when the spectator starts dealing.

If you want to be sure to find the juncture at the crimp of the index, you can put a small, loose paper clip at the lower end. This will force the juncture to stay wide and accessible at the upper end. I don't use it because I don't find it necessary.

The patter should be pertaining to "trying to photograph a thought," etc. I hope you agree with me that this is certainly an off-beat, and easily remembered (by the audience) card effect.

1-2-3 ACES

RECENTLY I was reminded of a juggling type move I used to do when I was just a kid. I used it for the appearance of a selected card. While toying with it, I thought of using it for a four-ace routine. I came up with a routine that's a fooler and is interesting to watch. I've been using it ever since.

The only problem is, it's going to be "murder" to explain on paper. It's not particularly easy to do; keeping it neat looking, anyway. You have to be able to do the double-cut and faro shuffle, although the shuffle need not be "perfect" at all.

In order to keep this confined to a reasonable amount of space, I have to assume that there are certain things you can do without my explaining them. I don't usually do that, I know—but if you *don't* know these things, in this case, you really shouldn't be attempting this effect.

Display the four aces and then place them into the deck, apparently losing them. This is the first thing I'm assuming you know how to do. Control the aces to the top. I'll only suggest that no matter which control you use, always do a couple of jog shuffles, retaining the aces, of course.

Now, the object is to reverse the four aces on top with an indifferent card face down on top of them, as cover. You may have your own methods for accomplishing this, but I'll tell you (or try to) how I do it; and then a suggestion or two.

Secure a left little finger break under the four aces. Take the deck from above in the right hand; the thumb retaining the break. Now you're going to do sort of an inverted double-cut. The left fingers undercut about half the deck and turn it face up *as* it's brought to the top. (See Fig. 114) to see this near completion. As this is done, say "No ace here . . ." The deck is squared, but the break is still held by the right thumb.

Now the left fingers undercut *to* the break and turn this half face up, but it is not put onto the cards in the right hand. *As* the left hand turns it face up (the thumb just flips it over), the left fingers push outward on the rear card, which tends to spread some of the rear cards to the right. The object is to separate the rear card from the others just a bit.

As this is done, you say, "No ace here (indicating the card at the face of this half), and no ace here on top (indicating the rear card)." To see the situation at this moment, (See Fig. 115).

The right-hand half is pushed *between* this rear card (4S in the figure) and the rest of the left-hand cards. (See Fig. 116). And square the deck. Now pull some cards from the *center* with the right hand, as per the Hindu Shuffle (See Fig. 117), and place on top—"And no ace here. They're all lost somewhere in the deck."

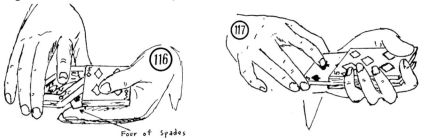

Four of Spades

That's done it! If you turn the deck face down now, you've reached the goal. There's an indifferent card, face down, on top, and the four aces are reversed directly beneath it. I'd suggest that you go over this description once more, with cards in hand.

I've broken it down into steps for you, but it's actually done as a blend of action, one step immediately leading into the other. It must look as if you're simply cutting the deck and showing that there are no aces in sight. And done correctly and neatly, it takes no more than a second or two.

That's how I do it. If you like, you can do the exact same thing, except—when you undercut the second half, place it face up to the top, the same as the first half. Square the face up deck, and either do a double-cut, bringing the face card to the rear, or—simply spread a few face cards, showing no aces, and nonchalantly place one of them to the rear. Do the Hindu Shuffle cut in either case— and you're in the same position.

Okay; the deck is face down, and you're ready to continue. "To make sure the aces are really lost, I'll give the deck another couple of shuffles." Do one or two jog shuffles, retaining the top five cards. If you do this neatly, there's no need to be afraid of premature spreading of the face up aces.

"And—the fairest shuffle you can give a deck of cards." Here you do a faro shuffle. Try to do an "out" shuffle—that is, the top card remains on top. Though it doesn't really matter. Try for the "out" butt; if it happens to be an "in" butt (where the top card becomes second from top)—let it go. Be careful when you square; don't allow the face up aces to be seen.

You don't have to worry about the cut for the shuffle, and only the top few cards of each half have to interlace properly. If you like, do one more jog shuffle, retaining the top nine or ten cards— and you're all set.

If you did an "out" butt, you'll have two indifferent face down cards on top, covering the first face up ace. If you did an "in" butt, then there are three face down cards. Patter: "I'm going to find each ace for you in a strange way. And each one, by the count of three. Watch."

As you talk, secure a break above the first face up ace; that is, under either the two or three top cards, according to the faro you did. Now do a regular double-cut (bringing the top cards to the bottom), counting "one, two, three," as you do it. This brings the first ace into view, face up on top of the deck. (And also gets rid of the two or three indifferent cards.)

I'm assuming you know the double-cut, but here's a real fast description: Deck is held from above, thumb retaining break (as when you started to reverse the aces). Left fingers undercut half the deck and bring it to the top. (You don't turn it face up this time.) Count "one" and square, retaining the break. Now undercut *half* the cards up to the break, bring them to the top, counting "two." Finally, undercut up to the break and bring those cards to the top, counting "three."

All right; deal the top face up ace to the table. Now the remaining three aces are face up on top, with one indifferent face down card covering each one.

These three aces are revealed by starting with the deck face up and doing three odd-looking cuts. Each time, when the deck is turned face up, you have to secure a left little finger break above the top (rear) indifferent card. I want to do this as smoothly and quickly as possible.

I use the "kick" move that I described in "The 'Kick' Double-Lift." Do the "get-ready" as I explained there. Now do the "kick" as at the same time, the left thumb goes under the deck and flips it face up. (You'll find that the thumb flipping the deck over *automatically* "kicks" that top card.) The right hand holds the deck from above as the deck turns face up, and the tip of the left little finger can easily pull down on the exposed corner and secure the break.

Again, this is done in one fluid action. All right; the deck is face up and you've secured a break above the bottom or rear card. Hold the deck from above, in the right hand; the thumb retaining the break.

You'd better follow this with cards in hand. The right fore-finger tip lifts (at the front end) and kicks about a third of the deck of the left. (See Fig. 118). The left hand takes this packet, still face up, and holding it down on the palm, carries it to the bottom and *takes* the "broken" indifferent card onto its face. (See Fig. 119). Notice that the left fingertips actually grab the card. In almost the same action, the left thumb flips this packet face down. As you do this, count "one."

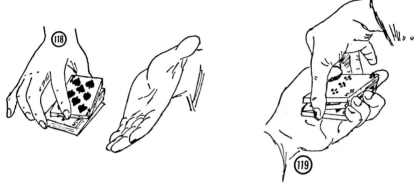

The right forefinger now lifts and kicks half the remaining right-hand cards to the left (as before). This packet is held by the left fingers (See Fig. 120) for a split second, as the right hand, using the cards it holds, flips it face down onto the left-hand cards. (See Fig. 121). And, count "two".

Now, and this is hard to describe, the right hand brings its cards directly above (about five or six inches) the left-hand cards. Stick the left thumb straight up. (See Fig. 122). Now, don't just drop, but lightly toss the right-hand cards straight down, so that the left underside of the packet hits the left thumb. This causes the right-hand cards to do an immediate flip-over. (See Fig. 123). The left thumb immediately grasps this top half to keep it from falling or spreading.

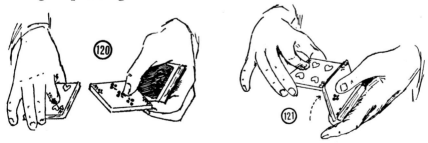

You'll have to try this a few times to acquire the "knack." This magically brings the second ace into view, face up on top, at the count of "three." Deal this ace onto, or near, the first one.

Turn the deck face up again, as I've explained, securing the
break over the rear indifferent card. Do exactly as for the preceding
ace, except with the last face up third of the deck. This is really
the same thing, but I want it to *look* a little different.

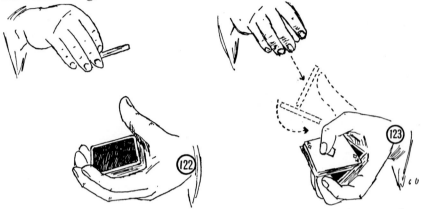

So, for the count of "three," this time, the left thumb is up, but
pointing slightly to the right. The right hand holds its packet to
the right, and slightly above the left hand. It tosses its packet sideways, to the left, onto the left-hand cards.

If the right-hand packet is held slightly slanted, before the toss
—again, the left thumb will act as the fulcrum, causing the packet
to do a fast flip-over. (See Fig. 124) to see the situation just before the right hand releases its packet.

Deal this ace down to join the other two. Say "I'll find the last
ace for you in slow motion."

Repeat exactly for this last ace as for the preceding two. This
time, however, place that last packet into the left fingertips. (See
Fig. 125). Pause for a moment as you say, "Watch; in slow motion."

Flip this packet face down onto the left-hand cards with the
right fingers; do it *slowly*. As the last ace comes into view, count
"three."

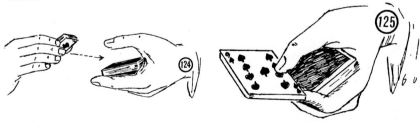

Deal this ace to the table to join the others; leave the deck on
the table also—to end.

Afterthoughts:—Well, that's about the best I can do to explain this. You'll have to put in some practice time.

Aside from the control and reversal of the four aces, the most important part is the grabbing of the "broken" indifferent card during the first cut—for all but the first ace. Don't particularly try to hide this; if it's done smoothly and quickly, it looks like you're turning the packet face down with a slight dramatic gesture. Remember that the left thumb flips the packet over immediately, after grabbing that card and the right hand (and its cards) hide the fact that the face card of that packet is changing.

If you're interested in how I control the four aces to the top at the beginning, I usually use Ed Marlo's "Simple Shift," from his book, *The Cardician.*

ABOUT FACES

M Y FRIEND, Jerry Lubin, did this effect for me, asking if I could come up with an ending for it. Although the mathematical principle on which it's based is an old one, he assured me that he had independently devised the version he was using.

I don't ordinarily 'dig' mathematical methods of locating selected cards, but I played with this for a while. I came up with more than just the ending.

I've been using it for some time now, and it's a fooler. I even fooled Jerry with it and then blackmailed him into giving me permission to use it here.

I've contributed the use of the key cards and the entire 'goof' ending idea. Without these, it's a very easy trick to perform. With them, it will take some work on your part. I have been accused before, of taking a simple thing and making it difficult and complicated. Well, that may be so—but, by the same token, I feel that I change a simple puzzle into something laymen will talk about; into a piece of magic, in other words. Remember too, that it's the entertainment value I'm after.

All right; have a deck shuffled. Take it back and shuffle it some more. In so doing, spot the top and bottom cards. These will be your keys. The way I usually do it is: I spot the bottom card during a riffle shuffle. I shuffle that to the top with an overhand shuffle. Then I do another riffle retaining the top card and spotting the new bottom card. I finish with a shuffle or cut, leaving top and bottom intact. You needn't remember which is where; just remember the two cards.

Place the deck, face down, onto the table. Tell one of your spectators to cut the deck into two approximately equal halves, then to cut each half into two approximately equal halves. In other words, the deck is cut into four about-equal packets. I usually manage it so that the packets containing my key cards are at the ends of the row. This isn't essential, so long as you keep track of them. But for explanation purposes, let's assume that the key packets are at the ends.

Start to patter along numerological lines; numbers play a large part in our lives, and so on. As you talk, you pick up, shuffle quickly, and replace, each packet. When you shuffle the packet which has a key on top, *retain* that top card. The next two packets are shuffled legitimately; and the last packet, the one with the key at the bottom, is shuffled so that the key is brought to the top, and kept there.

Do this nonchalantly and without looking, if you can. Also try to make it look as if each packet is being shuffled in the same way. When you're finished, you have a key card at the *top* of each end packet.

Tell Spectator A to pick up one of the center packets, one *without* a key. Spectator B picks up the other center packet (one without a key). Tell each spectator to count the cards in his packet. They can do this either behind their backs or under the table—or, as you turn your back. The important thing here is for them to count correctly. Stress this—perhaps with the patter idea that numerology is an *exact* science, etc., and they *must* count correctly.

When they've counted the cards in their respective packets, say that ordinarily, in numerology, you'd add their birthdays—year, month and day—down to a single digit—but since you don't want to get personal, you'll do the same with the numbers they've just arrived at.

"So—if the number you're now thinking of consists of two digits, please add the digits to each other, until you arrive at a single digit. For example, if your number is 11, one and one is 2. If it's 16, 1 and 6 equal 7, etc."

Each of your spectators *must* have *more* than nine cards in his packet in order for the effect to work. You must make sure of this when the deck is cut into four packets, originally. No problem; just get them about equal and each one will have at *least* ten cards.

Therefore—each spectator, at this point, will *have* to add the two digits of his number. Of course, at no time do they tell you what their numbers are. When they indicate that they're now thinking of single-digit numbers, tell each one to count down to *that* number in his packet. He's to remember the card at that position and *leave* it at that position.

This is the old mathematical principle I mentioned. Each thought-of card is now *tenth* from the *bottom* of each spectator's packet. The way I saw this originally—each spectator now placed a tabled packet *onto* his packet. This kept each selection at tenth from bottom. To my mind, this was a bit obvious. Now you can do it this way:—

Tell one spectator to cut one of the tabled packets into two halves. He places the packet that contains his card onto the *top* half of the cut tabled packet. (In other words, his packet goes directly *onto* one of your keys.) Then he completes this by placing the original bottom section of the tabled packet onto all. All that's happening, and what you patter about, is that the packet containing his card is buried into the center of the tabled packet. The other spectator does the same thing, using the remaining tabled packet.

Now have each spectator pick up his half deck and cut it (straight cuts) as often as he likes. Tell one spectator to take the other's half deck, turn either half *face up* and do one *riffle shuffle*, shuffling a face down half into a face up half. He now cuts the shuffled deck (straight cuts, again) as often as he likes.

Take the deck and patter to the effect that there is obviously no way in which you could find the thought-of cards. (This should certainly be taken to be a true statement.) But, having used numerology, there's just a possibility that you may be able to do so.

"And incidentally, in order to be a magician, it's necessary to learn how to quickly straighten out a deck that has been shuffled as to face up and face down. First—you can see that your cards are completely lost in the deck."

Here, you spread the cards looking for one of your key cards. When you find it, keep spreading, counting the key card as *one*, and counting *only face up cards*, to the *eleventh* one. This will be one of the selections! Remember it, and finish the spreading, of course. Try to do this without hesitating; you're simply spreading the cards once to show that a selected card is there, somewhere—and that the deck is thoroughly mixed.

Now turn the deck over and do the same thing. Only this time, when you pass the selected card, keep a step or break there. Turn the deck over again, *retaining* that break above the (now) face down selected card.

"Now watch how quickly I straighten out the deck." Here we come to a problem. The object is to straighten out the entire deck, *except* the two selections. There are a few ways to do this; the problem is to describe them! I'll do the best I can, but you'll have to use your imagination, and apply your knowledge.

The method I use most often, is what I believe is commonly known among magicians as the 'slop shuffle.' You start spreading cards, from the top of the deck, from one hand to the other. You spread all face up (or face down) cards (that happen to be on top; even one card) and then the hand that's taking the cards turns over to take face down (or face up) cards; then it turns over again, and so on. (See Fig. 126). This hand takes cards under its thumb and under its fingers alternately, as it turns. (See Fig. 127). If you do this all the way through the deck, the cards will be either all face up or all face down.

But—when you come to the face up selected card, you handle it *as if it were a face down card*. And when you come to the face down selection, over which you're still holding a break, you *treat it as a face up card*.

This is *not* easy. At first it's almost like patting your head with one hand while you make circles on your stomach with the other! It can get confusing. You'll just have to practice it until it comes easily.

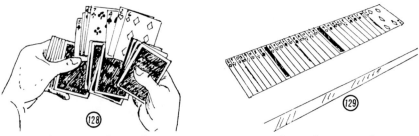

Don't worry about the spectators seeing a face down card among the face up group, or vice versa—as you do this. They'll be confused at this point, and it might be a good idea if *you* act confused. You might use a patter line like, "I'm going to keep practicing this until I get it right."

Another method I sometimes use, is the step-up. I step up all the face down (or face up) cards as I spread. (See Fig. 128). Again, handle the face up selection as a face down card, and the face down selection, as a face up card. When you've spread through the entire deck, strip out all the face down (or face up) cards and turn them properly, so the deck faces one way.

Whichever method you use, immediately do a wide *face up* ribbon spread on the table (See Fig. 129), saying, "See how I made them all face one way?" Pause, "Oh, oh, I goofed with two cards."

Take out the two face down cards, one in each hand. Ask for the names of the thought-of cards, and then turn up those you're holding, displaying the two thought-of cards!

Afterthoughts:—The mathematical principle is one which I'm sure you know. The thing you'll have to practice is the straightening of the deck while holding a break and while thinking of reversing the two selections. It will take practice.

The reason for the spreading and spotting the selections before I start straightening, is twofold: First, I don't want to have to do any counting *as* I'm straightening the deck.

And, second—if I spot one selection, turn over, holding a break and then *do* start straightening, looking for my key, and counting, etc.—there's the possibility of this second key being near the end of the spread. If this were so, I'd have to continue my count (to eleven) back at the beginning of the spread. And—it would be too late; I've already straightened that card, and lost it. I hope you can follow all this.

Of course, if you want to make this easier, you can simply cull out the two cards and then do any reverse you want. I do it as described. And, using the key cards as I explained, makes it appear impossible for you to know, or find, the two cards.

At first, I tried placing the key cards at the bottom of the spectators' packets (then I had to count to the *tenth* card)—but this created the problem of making sure the spectators didn't reverse the cards as they counted, etc. The way it is now, they can even shuffle their packets before they count.

It goes without saying, of course, that you have to practice this until you're at ease with the whole thing. The placing of the keys; the instructions to the spectators for the counting, cutting and shuffling; the spreading to locate the selections, and finally, the straightening of the deck leaving the selections reversed.

And—it takes much less time to perform this than to explain it.

FAVORITE ACES AND KINGS

IN MY last book, *My Favorite Card Tricks*, I included a routine from my One-Man Parade (Linking Ring—Vol. 44, No. 3), called, "Aces Only—With Kings." I said then that this was *one* of my favorites from the Parade.

Since that book appeared, many magicians have told me that they were glad I included it. Some of them had missed it in the Linking Ring and besides, they felt that they appreciated it more when taken out from among the other routines based on the same idea.

Anyway, that was *one* of my favorites from that Parade; and I've decided to include *the* favorite in this book.

You must be able to do a perfect "in" (where top and bottom cards are lost) faro shuffle and the double-cut, in order to present this routine. The effect is that the four aces are lost in the deck and then found by spelling them, a card for each letter. The kings appear mysteriously, and then *they* are used for some amazing finger-flinging.

I'll describe this in detail, so it will appear to be much longer than it actually is.

As you're removing the four aces from the deck, set the kings as follows: KC—10th; KH—11th; KD—14th; and KS—16th; all from the *face* of the deck.

Remember CHSD order, and then reverse the KS and KD. Another way to set the kings is to place the KC at the face, followed by the KH. Then place the KD and KS into 5th and 7th position respectively. Then, after removing the aces, shuffle or run nine cards from top to bottom! This places the kings correctly.

In both *My Favorite Card Tricks* and the Linking Ring Parade, I explained just how I set the kings *as* I'm searching for, and removing, the aces. I don't want to take the space to repeat it here. It's easy enough for you to look it up, if you're interested enough to do so.

The aces are placed face up on the table in the same suit order —CHDS, and you work backward from spade to club. Hold the deck face down and spread it from hand to hand in order to get a break over the four bottom cards.

Square the deck, holding the break with the left little finger-tip. Place the AS, face down, on top of the deck. As you patter about losing the aces one at a time, the right hand takes the deck from above, right thumb retaining the break at the bottom. Do a forefinger kick-off of the top half of deck (See Fig. 130); left hand places this half to the bottom, left little fingertip going into the break. Now double-cut to the break. This places the AS fifth from the top. Show that there are no aces on top or bottom.

Secure a break over the bottom card. Place the AD on top and repeat the cut and double-cut, just as you did for the AS. This brings the AD to second from the top.

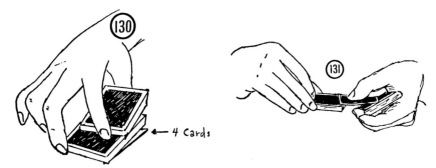

For the AH—cut the top half of the deck to the table. Place the AH face down onto this half. Drop the remaining half deck onto this, forming a step as you do. Pick up the deck, secure a break at the step, and double-cut to the break. This brings the AH back to the top. The patter while doing this: "Let's make sure the AH is lost by placing it here in the center of the deck, and cutting the deck a few times. . . ."

Now, holding the deck in your hands, put the AC on top, face down. Cut the top half of deck into the left hand, and with the left thumb run (or take) four cards, one by one, from the top of the right-hand half onto the left-hand half. (See Fig. 131). As you do this, say, "I'll *really* bury the AC."

Drop all the right-hand cards onto the left-hand cards, holding a break. Double-cut to the break. This places the AC fifth from top, with the AH directly under it. (I'm telling you where the aces should fall only so that you can check yourself as you learn this. There's certainly no reason to worry about where the aces fall when you're performing. This entire thing will work automatically, if you follow my instructions implicitly.) Show that there are no aces on top or bottom.

At this point, I usually say, "Now you know the aces are lost in the deck. But to assure you of that fact, I'll give the deck the fairest shuffle possible." Now give the deck one perfect "in" faro shuffle. Patter: "What I've tried to do is to place the aces, after all that shuffling, so that each ace will spell out, one card for each letter. This may not seem to be so difficult until you realize that each ace spells with a different amount of letters. For example, clubs has five letters, diamonds has eight, etc. Look, instead of talking about it, why don't I just do it for you? I'll spell the AC first."

From the top of the deck, dealing the cards face down, one by one, and one on top of the other, spell out a-c-e-o-f-c-l-u-b-s. Always name the ace you're going to spell before you spell it. And, I usually repeat each word after I've spelled it.

Place the card that falls on the final "s" face down on the table, near the spectator. Ask him to turn over the card to see if it's the AC. This is just for misdirection and time. Because you must reverse (turn face up) the card that is now second from the top (AH). This is not absolutely necessary; you can do the routine without reversing the AH—but I'm describing it the way I perform it.

The way to reverse the AH, *as* the spectator is turning over the AC, is to deal off the top card with the left thumb. The right hand takes this card from above, fingers on outer end, thumb on inner

end. Left thumb pushes off the next card (AH) and the right hand uses the left edge (or side) of its card as a lever to flip over the second card; and immediately, in the same motion, drops the card it's holding onto it. The left thumb acts as the fulcrum in aiding the AH to turn over. (See Fig. 132). If done properly, that is— quickly, smoothly and without looking—it can't be seen. (There is a complete description of this move on Page 266 of *Close-Up Card Magic*.)

The spectator, meanwhile, has turned over the AC. Place this, face up, above the face down spelled-card packet. "You may think that I've got all the aces placed where I want them. To prove I haven't, I'll shuffle these *remaining* cards."

Leaving the AC and its packet on the table, give the remaining cards a perfect "in" butt. The cut here is easy because the KS is at dead center. Cut so the KS is at the face of the top half. Be careful when squaring after the shuffle—you don't want to expose the face up AH prematurely.

"To prove that everything is open and above board, I'll spell the other black ace, the AS, face up. Watch!" Turn the deck face up and, starting a new packet alongside the first one, spell out the AS, leaving the spelled cards face up. The AS will fall on the final "s." Place it alongside the AC and above its own spelled packet, forming a row of aces.

As soon as the AS is placed on the table, spread some cards at the face of the deck, saying, "And there's no other ace in sight." This is an excuse to give you a reason for placing or moving *two* cards from the *face to the rear.* Do it nonchalantly and don't make any effort to hide it. Of course, you could double-cut two from face to rear, if you like—I do it as explained.

Turn the deck face down. "Just to assure you that I have no idea where the other two aces are—I'll even shuffle these remaining cards."

Do another "in" butt. You'll be working with an odd number (31) of cards here. The smaller half (15) must be cut from the top and shuffled *into* the bottom larger (16) half. You'll find this quite easy with a small amount of cards.

Say, "This time I'll spell the AH, but—I'll go a step further. Not only will I spell it, but to show you the extent to which these cards are under my control, I'll make the AH reverse itself by magic!"

Snap your fingers or riffle the ends for effect, and holding the deck face down spell out the AH starting a new face down packet of spelled cards. Deal the card on the final "s" slowly and the face up AH is the next card. Place this above its spelled packet.

"Well, there's only one ace to go, the AD. I only have a few cards left, but I'll even shuffle *these* just to assure you that I couldn't know where the ace is."

You have 19 cards left. Give these a perfect "in" butt. The smaller half (9) butting into the bottom larger (10) half. Now spell out the AD, holding the cards face down but dealing each one *face up,* and forming a new face up spelled-card packet.

The AD will fall on the final "s"—place it above its packet. (See Fig. 133). As soon as you place the AD, drop the remaining few cards (6) still in your hands *onto the first spelled packet* (the AC packet). At the same time, turn the second packet (AS packet) face down.

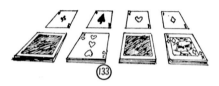

After a pause, pick up the face card of the AD face up spelled-card packet (the KD) and tapping it on the AD, say, "Now here's a coincidence; here's the king to match this ace. But, if I were to tap each of these cards with the AD, it's no longer coincidence—it's magic!"

During this patter, you tap the face up KD once on each of the remaining face down packets, then replace the KD to the face of the AD face up packet. Then turn up the top card of each face down packet, showing the king to match its ace!! Leave these kings face up on their respective packets, and give this a moment to sink in.

You can end right here, if you like—it's certainly strong enough. But I've taken it a step further, and I, personally, always continue. Patter: "These kings are amazing; they really are. Look, I'll lose them into the deck any old way."

While talking, turn the first three kings face down onto their packets. Leave the KD packet as is—face up. The aces are left in a face-up horizontal row, in CSHD order; just as you spelled them.

As you talk about losing the kings, do this: Turn the entire KD packet face down *onto* the packet to its left—that is, the AH packet. Just flip it over like the page of a book. The spectators can see the KD obviously being lost.

Pick up the three (now) packets from left to right. The first one going onto the second and the combined first and second going onto the combined third and fourth. Pick up and square the deck. "Let's make sure they're lost, just as I did with the aces!" Give the deck a perfect "in" butt. After squaring, you can show that there's no king on top or bottom, by showing the top and bottom cards only. Look at one spectator and say, "I don't think you trust me, do you? Look, I'll give the deck another shuffle."

Do another perfect "in" butt. You have a key for your cut here. The KD will be the top card of the lower half, if you cut correctly. After the shuffle the KD is the top card.

Do a false cut, or a double-cut, retaining the top stock. Take the top card and tap it on the AD, saying, "After all that shuffling, if I tap *any* card on say the AD, it automatically becomes the KD!" Turn it face up and place it onto and overlapping the AD.

Do an overhand shuffle, adding *two* cards to the top. The KC is now fifth from the top of the deck. (When you do the overhand shuffle, you must retain the top 17 or 18 cards.)

Give the deck a false cut or double-cut (or just drop it onto the table after the overhand shuffle) and say, "Or, if I want to, I can just turn up the top card, and *whatever* it is, it will find say— the KC!"

Turn up the top card and place it face up onto the table. Now, whatever that card is, you can get to the KC. I explained this idea in "Any Four Of A Kind" in *My Favorite Card Tricks.* So, I assume you know it. If you turn up a 5-spot, you simply count five *including* the turned-up card. This brings you right to the KC.

If you turn up a 4-spot, count four *without* including the turned-up card. If it's a 3-spot, don't include it, count 3 and turn up the next card. *All* the other cards *spell* with either 3, 4 or 5 letters (you can spell three instead of counting 3, if you like). So you'd spell the turned-up card, including it or not, and turning up the next card —accordingly. Of course, whatever the card is, you must use it to get to the KC without hesitation.

All right; get to the KC; tap it face down on the AC, then turn it face up to display. Leave it face up on, and overlapping, the AC. Display each king the same way, after it's located.

Place all the counted or spelled cards to the bottom of the deck. The KH is now on top! Give the deck one jog shuffle, retaining the top 12 or 13 cards. Produce the KH any way you like, so long as you don't lose the top stock while doing so.

Indicate the AH first (I do this with all of them, making it appear as if I can make *any* king appear whenever I like. The order in which they do appear is easy to remember. The end aces first, then the two center ones; reds first in each case. The *aces* are originally spelled in CSHD order, of course.)

The method I'd suggest for the KH is dropping the deck causing it (the KH) to turn face up. There's a detailed description of the proper way to do this on Page 71 of *Close-Up Card Magic*.

Shuffle the deck, again adding two cards to the top. In each case where you have to add two cards to the top—you can do it via the double-cut. I prefer the jog shuffle method because the audience *must* agree that it's impossible to control anything that way.

"Well, I'm missing only the KS. Since I started this as a spelling trick, why don't I finish it the same way? I'll spell the KS." Spell it out slowly, and it will fall on the final "s." Tap it on the AS, turn it face up, etc.—and finish!!! (See Fig. 134).

Afterthoughts:—Well, that's it! It took some explaining, and although I wouldn't call it a quickie exactly, it's not as long as it appears to be.

As I said in the text, you can end after spelling the aces and showing the matching kings. I never do. If you continue with the kings, as if you're *just* making it all up, it gives the impression that you can do just about *anything* with cards!

I also *never* omit the reversing of the AH. You're a few steps ahead of your audience with this, and it *has* to make them sit up and take notice! Of course, you've got to do the reversal smoothly.

Perform this entire thing well and your audiences will probably consider you the best card handler that ever lived!

This is one of my favorite routines, and if you give it the time and practice it deserves, and get it working smoothly—I'm sure it will become one of your favorites, too.

STABBED IN THE PACK

THE TITLE really belongs to J. Benzais. He saw me do a card-tossing effect and asked me if he could contribute it to the New Jinx. I said yes, and he did. He used the title, Stabbed In The Pack. He also made an estimation effect out of it which was not the effect I did for him.

Anyway, it started quite a controversy. Letters poured in exclaiming that it couldn't be done, and so forth. After some months of this, I decided to send the effect *as I performed it* for years, to Bill Madsen of the New Jinx.

I called it, "Will The Real Stabbed In The Pack Please Stand Up!" and it appeared in the November, 1966 issue of the New Jinx. It was, more or less, a tongue-in-cheek write-up, but it *did* describe exactly how I do the thing. So, because I'm basically quite lazy, I'm including it here just as it appeared there, with only a few changes.

I had also written a letter to The New Jinx (June, 1966) in which I mentioned some presentation ideas. I'll use excerpts from this in the Afterthoughts, and other excerpts as I need them in the text. I told you I was lazy!

The effect is that a card is selected and lost in the deck. The magician takes one card, leaving the deck on the table. He *tosses the indifferent card into* the deck and shows that it has landed *right next* to the selected card!

Now—I said in that letter, "I don't use this effect any more. It's the kind of thing that should be done *all the time or not at all!*" What I was referring to, was the tossing of the card. This is not easy; but once you've mastered it and do it often enough, either performing or just practicing, you'll rarely miss. (See Afterthoughts.)

All right; a card is selected and you control it to the *bottom* of the deck. Show the top card, saying, "And here's your card." When this is denied, place the face down deck on the table *almost horizontally* with a corner facing a bit toward you. (See Fig. 135). It's easier for the tossed card to enter the deck this way. Still holding the top (indifferent) card, say, "Oh well, let me trust to luck."

Now, although I know that a picture is worth a thousand words —it's difficult to draw a picture of a card in flight. So clear your mind and nasal passages and read *carefully* and I'll try to describe exactly how I toss the card into the deck (in less than a thousand words). And if you think this is tough, wait 'till I try to describe the ending!

Hold the card face up as you would normally hold a card you wanted to toss. I hold it horizontally with the right thumb and first and second fingers at the upper right-hand corner. (See Fig. 136).

Step away from the table so that you're about three feet from the *deck*. The reach of your arm as you go into the toss will bring the card and your hot little hand to about *one foot* from the deck.

So, if you're taller than I (and who isn't) and have longer arms,

you can stand, say, four feet from the deck. The point is, the card is released when it is approximately one foot away from the deck, give or take a few inches. All this, of course, is done in one smooth action, and it appears as if the card travels much farther than it actually does. It's the same principle as the hand-to-hand spring or waterfall shuffle. The illusion created is that the spread of cards is much longer than it actually is.

Now then, if you toss the card *directly* at the deck, by some rule of nature (centrifugal force? Inertia? Gravity? Einstein's Theory Of Relativity? I don't know!) the card *must* fly *over* the deck and continue on it's merry way. So you *must* bounce it off the table top into the deck. But, not too close to the deck, like an inch or so. That's not enough leeway. The best you'll get then is—the card will either slide under the entire deck, or, enter at only one or two cards from the bottom. That's no good. So—bounce it at about *four or five* inches from the deck. (See Fig. 137).

Now here's a most essential point: If you're towering above the deck and bounce that card four or five inches in front of the deck, it will bounce right *over* the deck!

You should be *crouching* when you toss. You'll find this to be the most natural looking way to do it anyway. In other words, the card shouldn't be more than, say, two or three inches above the deck's level when it leaves your hand.

Toss it fairly forcefully (you'll find the proper (for you) speed only with practice) and after your 10th or 15th attempt, you may get that d--n card into the deck.

"Seriously folks," if done properly, you'll surprise yourself. The card enters the deck (with practice, near center each time) as easily as a lit cigarette enters your favorite pull. It looks great; the card travels quickly and (seemingly) quite far, and stops *dead* in the deck.

Don't use a deck that's crimped or bent from here to backwards; read the preceding few paragraphs again, paying attention this time —and practice, baby, practice!

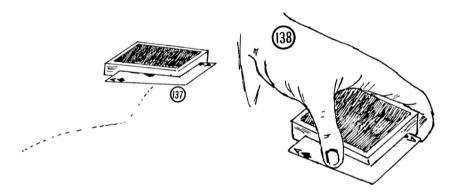

Now then—the all-important ending. The selected card has been controlled to the bottom of the deck. And incidentally, if you can't control a card to the bottom so that it doesn't *look* like you've controlled a card to the bottom—I'm sorry we've wasted each other's time—but this effect is not for you!

Now toss that card into the deck as explained. Return to your seat and ask for the name of the selected card. If everything has gone as planned, the deck is facing you horizontally and the tossed card is protruding, face up, toward you, from about the center of the deck.

When the card is named, do this: (I use my left hand as described; either hand will do.) Place your left thumb onto the protruding (tossed) card so that part of the fleshy part of the ball of the thumb also rests on the horizontal near sides of the *top* half of the deck. (*Oh* boy!)

At the *same time,* the remaining four fingers go under the *entire* deck at the *far* side. (See Fig. 138). This means that the four fingertips are resting on the bottom (chosen) card.

Start to *gently* pull the left hand away from you and away from the *lower* half of the deck. That is—the left thumb presses the top half of the deck against the left fingers (at the point where they meet the palm); leave the tossed card where it is, and the *left fingertips also move the bottom card along with the top half*. (See Fig. 139) for partial side view.

Repeat the name of the selected card and *slam* this top half of the deck, *face up*, onto the table. (See Fig. 140). I guess you could call this a "bass ackwards" slip-cut!

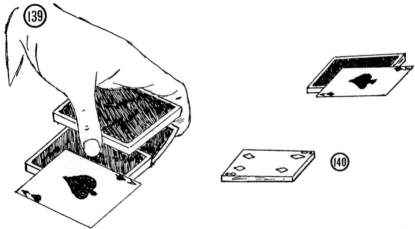

What it looks like and what your spectators see is that the cards above the tossed card are turned face up in one block; that's all. At least, that's what it looks like when *I* do it! Meaning, of course, that the tossed card obviously entered the deck just *under* the selected card. (Just be sure you don't make this *look* like a move.)

When you grab that top half of the deck, a *very light* pressure by the left fingertips will carry the bottom card along (actually, the weight of the cards alone is enough), and it simply coalesces with the top half. If more than one card leaves the bottom, it doesn't matter, since the selected card will still show when you slam the top half face up onto the table.

Start the move gently, but when you know that the bottom card is coming along as it should, move the hand quickly upward and away from the lower half (until the bottom card clears), and *slam* that top half face up onto the table.

Just remember that it *must* look simply as if you're turning the cards above the tossed card face up with a *slight* dramatic gesture—that's all!

Well, I told you this was a tough one to describe. Any time you see me around—drunk or sober—just ask me, and I'll do the darn thing for you! I can probably perform it about fifteen times in the time it takes to read what I've just written.

Afterthoughts:—As I said, I don't do this effect much any more. And, this is rarely so. Ordinarily I use and perform all the effects I write.

When I made my living doing table magic (that's over twenty years ago) I did this effect at almost every table. And I don't like to stand there with egg on my face; I *always* end my effects. On the rare occasions that the toss missed and the card landed in a spectator's lap, or stuck in his jacket, etc., I had a couple of "ad libs" ready that got laughs anyway.

Then I'd simply take the card and do it again; I never missed twice in a row! I always made sure that a spectator was opposite me, so that if I missed, the card landed on him; this was just in case, and set up my "ad lib."

Once you get the "feel" of the toss, however—and if you do it often enough—you won't have to worry about it.

And finally—I know that this can be done by simply pushing the indifferent card into the deck. But—it's the *tossing of that card* that your audiences will remember and talk about!

THE STRIP-OUT SLEIGHT

I'VE USED this sleight, and the routine that follows, for more years than I care to think about. The sleight itself is by no means a new idea. I believe that my method is easy, natural and convincing. Try it and judge for yourself.

Say you want to control the four jacks. Remove them, and pressure fan the deck in your left hand. Insert the jacks into the fan, one by one, for about one-third their length. Place them at intervals, starting from the bottom of the deck (left side of fan) and so that the fourth jack is about fifteen or twenty cards from the top (right side) of the fan. (See Fig. 141).

The right hand starts closing the fan from right to left. (See Fig. 142). As the fan closes, *press upward* on the top card of the deck with the left thumb. This will bevel the cards above the top jack in an upward direction. (See Fig. 143). Close the fan completely.

Grasp the deck at the inner end between your right thumb and fingers, in Hindu-Shuffle position. (See Fig. 144). I usually hold the deck vertically as shown in the figure, and with the back of deck facing the spectators. In this position, the right hand completely covers the irregular condition of the inner ends of the few top cards.

With the left forefinger (or all the fingers), slowly push the four protruding jacks down and flush. (The right little finger should be at the inner end to keep the jacks from pushing out other cards.)

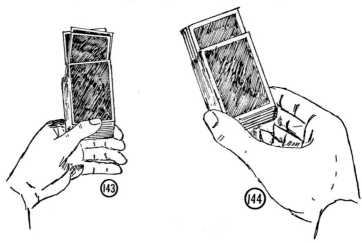

From the spectators' view, it appears as if they're going flush with the deck. Actually, they only go as far down as the beveled top cards. (See Fig. 145). To enhance the illusion, do a squaring motion with the left fingers, on the top edges of the cards.

Now do a Hindu Shuffle, but during the first movement, the

left thumb and second fingertip grasp up near the outer end of the deck. In this way, you actually grasp the protruding jacks and some of the beveled top cards *only*. The first movement of the Hindu Shuffle, therefore, strips out all the jacks with some cards above them. (See Fig. 146).

Continue the shuffle in the usual way and at its conclusion, the four jacks are at the bottom of the deck. I usually do one more Hindu Shuffle immediately, stripping out from the center (with my right hand) for the first movement. This, of course, keeps the bottom stock intact.

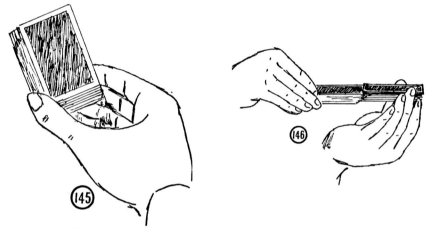

That's the move. I've really contributed very little to this except for the beveling of the top few cards *as* the fan is closed. This, however, makes it a much better move, to my mind. It eliminates the obvious step-up of those top few cards, which is how it was originally done and which I never liked.

Practice my way and I think you'll find it a quite natural-looking and easy-to-do control for four cards.

Now here's a routine utilizing The Strip-Out Sleight. For the record, call it

VICE TRIUMPHANT

I don't particularly care for "story" patter of this kind, although I guess I can hold my own in the patter department. Once in a while, I think it's all right. This is such an effect, though you can change the patter idea any way you like.

Remove the four jacks saying that they represent a gang of jewel thieves. The deck itself represents a 48-story hotel (clever?)

which the thieves intend to enter in order to steal some valuable diamonds.

Turn the deck *face up*, make the pressure fan and insert the jacks *face down*. The patter is that you're putting the jacks in reversed for easy identification. Do the Strip-Out Sleight which brings the face down jacks to the bottom of the face up deck.

Patter to the effect that the thieves were spotted by a guest who gave the alarm. The house detectives searched the hotel, but the thieves (jacks) had vanished.

This is how you show that the jacks are gone:—Hold the deck (face up, of course) in dealing position. Assuming you deal with your left hand, the left thumb spreads, say, eight to ten cards into the right hand. The right hand turns over, turning these few cards face down. (See Fig. 147). These are placed to the bottom of the deck where they coalesce with the four reversed jacks. The idea, of course, is that the cards are spread widely to show that there are no reversed cards among them.

Keep spreading cards and turning them face down to the bottom. Now, when you spread to an ace, leave the ace at the face of the deck, bringing the other cards to the bottom. Note the suit of the ace as you spread, reverse and bring to bottom a few more cards. This places the noted ace to the bottom.

Now, without pausing, spread *four cards only* and place them to the bottom *without reversing them*. Don't let this scare you. If you do it nonchalantly and without breaking rhythm, it will not be noticed.

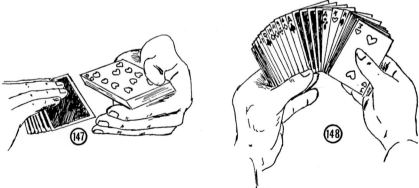

Again, without pausing, continue spreading until you reach another ace. Note its suit and turn the spread cards, *including* this ace, to the bottom. What this has accomplished is—you've placed four indifferent reversed cards between two known aces!

Continue spreading and reversing until you come to the first face down card. (Spread a few of these just to show that they're face down.) You've shown every(?) card and the reversed jacks have vanished. They really are on top of the deck, of course.

The patter now is that the hotel manager called in two ace detectives, the AC and the AS (name the aces you noted during the spreading). Riffle the ends of the deck to represent the two aces searching for the jacks. Spread the cards, *face up* in your hands, until you come to four face down cards with one of the named aces at each side. (See Fig. 148).

Place these six cards, in a spread, on the table as they are, the aces face up and the four cards between them, face down. Talk about the aces having succeeded, etc., as you turn the deck face down and get the four top cards ready for palming. Don't palm them yet.

Tell the spectator to check if the aces have really caught the jacks. Palm the four jacks *as* he turns over the four indifferent cards. Act surprised when you see the indifferent cards. You can either get the palmed jacks into your pocket and leave them there as you patter and show your hands empty for a moment—as I do; or—keep them palmed until you reach into your pocket and produce them.

Either way, say that the thieves must have escaped to their hideout, which is your pocket (of course). Produce the jacks from your pocket—to end!

Afterthoughts:—When I originally did this, I had from four to six diamond cards in my pocket before I started the routine. That way, when I produced the jacks from their hideout (my pocket), I could say, "And they had the loot (diamonds) with them," and bring out the 'diamonds.'

I don't bother with this any more, but you may like it—so I thought I'd mention it.

Don't overlook the idea of getting the four indifferent cards reversed between two *known* cards. I fool magicians with this even now, and I incorporated the idea in an effect called "Card Sandwich" in *Close-Up Card Magic*.

You don't have to use aces as the two detective cards. You don't even have to use like cards. You can use *any* two cards, as long as you name them before they're seen. So, you can say, "The hotel manager called in two famous detectives, the 8H and the 4C"—or what have you. This would be easier, since you wouldn't have to look for any particular card or cards. (Although I always manage to use a pair.)

There are, of course, many ways of controlling four cards to the top or bottom of the deck, one of the best of which, in my opinion, is Marlo's "Simple Shift"—as I mention in "1-2-3 Aces."

But, as I've told you before, I make it a habit to use certain moves with certain effects. I always use the Simple Shift for "1-2-3 Aces," but I always use my Strip-Out Sleight for "ViceTriumphant."

And finally, as far as reversing the four indifferent cards is concerned—and I know I keep repeating this 'ad boredom'—do it nonchalantly and without hesitation—that is, *naturally*—and you'll have no trouble with it.

TRAMPOLINE

Now I want to teach you two flourish type things to play with. They'll take some playing with, before you get them working. This one is simply the revelation of a selected card.

Assume you've controlled a chosen card to second from the top. Do this:—Holding the deck face down in your left hand in dealing position—deal the top three cards, one at a time, into your right hand in stepped order, lengthwise. The second card is dealt *under*, but stepped *above*, the first card. (See Fig. 149). The third card is dealt under, and stepped above, the second card. (See Fig. 150).

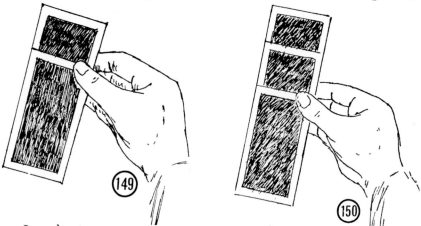

I can't give you exact measurements, but—expose a little less than half of the second card, and expose a bit less than that of the third card. Check the illustrations again.

Place these three cards onto the deck so that the second (center) card is flush with the deck proper. The deck should be squared. (See Fig. 151). Place the deck onto the table, keeping the three stepped cards in position. A long side of the deck is facing you.

Ask for the name of the chosen card. Now, you're going to press down on the ends of the two protruding cards with your forefingers. (See Fig. 152).

This is impossible to describe in print. Don't press down too sharply, or that center card will fly out any which way; which is an ending, anyway. Press down and *leave* the forefinger tips on the cards. In other words, don't *hit* the two cards and immediately remove the fingertips.

Also—it will work better if you think of letting the *left* forefinger tip touch its card just an instant *before* the right forefinger tip. If done correctly, the center card flips over (See Fig. 153), and *goes back* between the other two cards! The end result is as in (Fig. 154).

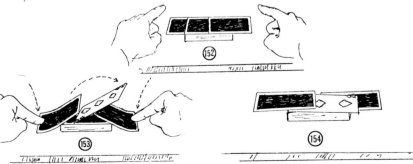

You'll notice that after the flip-over, the three cards have changed their order. The original top card is now third, and the original third card is now on top—the steps are in reversed order.

I can't describe this any better. You'll just have to play with it until you get the 'touch' or knack. Done correctly, it's an instant flip-over and an interesting revelation of a selected card.

Instead of dealing the three cards into your right hand in stepped order, you can pull back the top card, then pull back that *and* the next card, and finally push those two and the third card outward until the second card is flush with the deck. This puts the three cards in position. I do it by dealing as described.

Also—I usually control the selected card to the top. Then I show that the card is not among the top three by doing a double-lift. Then holding this card(s) face up, I use it to flip over the next card. This is dealt face up beneath (rear) of the double-lifted card(s). Then I flip over the next card and deal it face up *onto* the face of the right-hand cards. Now I flip all three (really four) cards face down onto the deck, and square. This shows that the selected card is not among the top three and at the same time, places it to second from top. Then do the 'trampoline' move—to end.

Afterthoughts:—If you can't seem to get the move working properly, you'll have to experiment with the distance of the steps and with the pressure of the forefinger tips. Those are the two important elements. You'll find that an almost easy touch of the forefinger tips does it. And—use a deck that isn't bent all out of shape.

Keep trying—it will surprise you when it works!

FLYING ACES

D ON'T give up on this one. Get it working properly and it will stay in your repertoire forever! Frankly, I didn't want to give this away—but since you've come this far with me, consider it a bonus.

Control the four aces to the top. Take any card, show it, and place it on top of the deck, over the aces. Mention the name of this card. Show that there is no ace at the bottom.

Hold the deck face down from above, in the right hand. Right thumb is at the *right* of the inner end. Second finger is at the *right* of the outer end. (See Fig. 155).

The right forefinger tip pulls back, into an almost buckled position, the top two cards. This is about as difficult to describe as anything in this book. I'll try, however. The right forefinger tip goes to the outer end, where it touches the second finger. With the ball of the fingertip, start to pull back the top card. (See Fig. 156).

It keeps moving back, pressing down and bringing along the second card. (See Fig. 157). The two cards are brought back to about the position shown in the figure. It is *not* necessary to bring them so far back as to actually leave a crimp in them. (The right thumb, of course, acts as the 'stop' causing the cards to buckle.)

Now, with a smart forward, or throwing motion—you'll find that you can shoot out the *second* card by releasing the pressure of the forefinger tip. The top card remains buckled as the second card shoots out. In other words the forefinger tip sort of lifts upward the slightest bit, taking the top card with it. This allows the second card to straighten itself out.

The force of the second card straightening, is not enough to cause the card to leave the deck. It's *that* force *combined* with the short back and forth throwing motion, that shoots out the card. It will take some practice; it's really just a wrist action. After a while, you'll shoot that card out up to three feet, or so. And, it causes a snap sound that adds to the effect. (The back and forth movement is actually, more or less, a sideways movement. It's similar to the movement you'd make shooing away a fly. That's the closest I can come to describing it.)

All right; if the card lands face up, everyone sees that it's an ace. If it lands face down, turn it up to display. Show that the top card is still the same indifferent card—ditto for the bottom card.

Repeat exactly for each ace. Done correctly, it's impossible to tell where the card is coming from and it's something audiences remember and talk about.

Afterthoughts:—Again, this is one of those things that requires just a bit of practice in order to acquire the knack. Once you do acquire it, it's easy to do.

Do the pull back of the two cards *as* you move the hand back in preparation for the throw. And, without pausing, do the throw. Or better still, do it as I do:—I show the top card and replace it. Then I get the deck into 'throw' position. *Now* I turn my hand, and the deck, to show the bottom card. *As* I turn my hand *back*, and the deck face down, I start to pull back the two cards with my forefinger. By the time the deck is face down, I'm set. I pull back my hand (in preparation for the throw) in a continuation of the turning down movement. Then I throw. It's all really one blend of movement.

I've tried this holding my hand so that the deck is vertical instead of horizontal. It will work as well, but there's too much chance of the spectator seeing that top card held back. Do it with the face of deck facing the table—you're better off that way. And—with some more practice, you can make the card flip over and land face up each time!

Also, you'll find that it's the *outer side* of the forefinger tip that does most of the work. And—after the second card has left, the forefinger is lying almost flush and crossways across the corner of the top card. (See Fig. 158). Of course, as soon as the second card leaves, let the top card straighten itself.

You can use this for the revelation of one or more selected cards, instead of the four aces. Be sure you *always* show the top and bottom cards before doing the flourish. And finally—you might want to practice holding a half deck in each hand and shooting out the second card of each half simultaneously!

Afterthought to Afterthought:—I started doing this this way after I wrote the above. It's really the same thing—but:—The aces are on top with one indifferent card on them.

Show that there's no ace on top or bottom. Now, hold the deck face down in the left hand. The left thumb riffles down on the outer left corners, asking a spectator to say, 'stop.'

When he does, the right hand takes the cards from above where he stopped you—in 'throw' position. Turn the hand up, showing that you were not stopped at an ace. "But watch"—and shoot out the second card as usual. Replace the half deck and show the same indifferent card at top and bottom. Repeat with three different spectators—or what have you.

This is a 'throw-off' because it seems as if the place at which you're stopped is important. Of course, it isn't.

As I said at the beginning of this—don't give up. After you've practiced a while and start doing it, you'll wonder why it seemed so difficult at first!

The Harry Lorayne
Magic Lecture

Harry Lorayne
doing Close-up Magic

THE CHOICE IS YOURS

This book was to have been completed after the last effect. But —Art Johnston showed Lou Tannen a gambling move, which Art said had been shown to him over thirty years ago.

Lou got all excited over it; did some checking, and so far as he could tell, it hasn't appeared in print before.

He insisted that I include it here. I made a deal with him; if I included the effect he liked, I could include another effect that I liked. He asked to see it, and said that if it fooled him, I could include it. That effect follows this one!

Now for the Lou Tannen—Art Johnston thing. It was vaguely familiar to me when Lou did it for me. I had seen it and played with it years ago.

It seems to have been used (still is, for all I know) in a gambling game that we used to call, "Bankers And Brokers" or just "Bundles," when I was a kid on the lower East Side of Manhattan.

The Banker would cut a shuffled deck into face down packets, and each player would put his money on the packet of his choice. (Whoever selected a packet with an ace at the face, became the new Banker.)

One packet was left for the Banker. Then the packets were turned face up and the highest card (between Banker and player) won. (There are no ties; the Banker always wins if the cards match.)

To present this quick effect, wait until you think your spectator is really watching you closely. (You're sitting at a table opposite him.) Give a little background of "Bankers And Brokers," as I've explained, and as you talk, get an ace to second from the bottom and a deuce or 3-spot at the bottom.

As you shuffle, make sure the spectator gets a glimpse of the face card. (I always use a deuce.)

Okay; place the deck face down, horizontally and slightly to your left, at the very edge of the table top. The long side of the deck is toward you.

Now cut a bit less than two thirds of the deck to the right. (I find that if there are more cards in that first pile, it facilitates the move, so I always leave a bit more than a third of the deck there.) Then cut these cards in half, placing the last pile to the right of the other two.

You now have three piles at the edge of the table. The one on your left is the original bottom, the one with a deuce at the face and an ace just above that.

Tell the spectator that he has first choice of a packet which he thinks has a high card at its face. Let him point to the one he wants. The idea, of course, is that the larceny in his heart will force him to select any one but the original bottom packet, since he knows it has a deuce at its face. (I'll explain what to do if he's kind of stupid or unobservant, and selects the bottom pile—in just a moment.)

When he indicates a pile, ask him how much he'd like to bet. (Say this with a smile, or with an attitude which let's him know that you're kidding and aren't betting 'for real.')

Whatever he says, point to the left pile (original bottom) and say, "All right; I'll take this one. Would you like to raise your bet?"

Since he now sees that you've selected the pile with the deuce at its face, he'll usually 'up' his bet. As soon as he does, say, "Well, I'm afraid you lose, because I've got an ace!"

As you say this, turn up the three piles, doing the following move:—You're going to turn the piles face up by turning them over *away* from you. (You can use either hand. For explanation purposes, let's use the left.)

Place your left hand on the original bottom pile, as in (Fig. 159). Slide the pile toward yourself slightly, and then start turning it away from you, as in (Fig. 160). The thumb automatically goes under the packet.

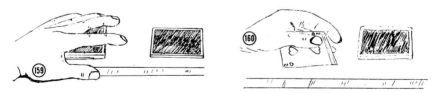

Now; if you apply very slight pressure with the left thumb, sliding the face card up and then against the palm, it will *remain in your hand,* as the remainder of the cards fall face up! (See Fig. 161) for view of the move at about mid-way.

Now (See Fig. 162), which illustrates the situation just as the pile has turned completely face up. (The left hand in this figure has been turned more toward you, just to show how the card is being held. Actually, the hand may be more palm down, and it never stops moving, anyway.)

As soon as this first pile is face up (actually, the left hand starts moving away from the pile even *before* it comes to a complete rest) and without a pause, the left hand moves to the second (center) pile, and simply places this stolen card *onto* it (See Fig. 163), *as* it turns this pile face up in *exactly* the same action.

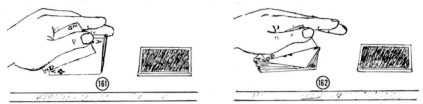

Then, and again, without pausing, the left hand moves to the third pile, and turns that up in the same way.

That's it. You've stolen the deuce from the face of the first pile, exposing the ace—and lost the deuce by placing it *onto* the second pile.

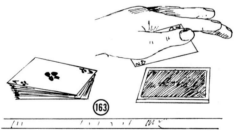

This stolen card is *not* palmed. Don't try to hide it completely. It's just held to your palm with the thumb. I guess if you have a very large hand, it *will* be covered, but it's not important.

One entire corner of the card is exposed when I do it, but it doesn't matter. What *does* matter, is that you do it in beat, and in a blend of action. Not quickly necessarily (not slowly, either)—but in beat, smoothly, and with no hesitations. Any exposed part of the stolen card will simply blend in with the back of the second pile, and shouldn't be seen.

It won't take you more than three or four tries to get this working smoothly. Remember, if it *feels* awkward, it will probably *look* awkward; so practice it. It will feel and look smooth in a surprisingly short while.

Of course, you realize that you must steal only *one* card (the deuce), otherwise the ace will be lost, too. If you want a 'hedge,' you can leave two (or three) aces behind that face deuce; then if two (or three) cards move, you'll still expose an ace. But, you're much better off practicing it until you're sure of stealing just the one card.

Now—what if your spectator selects the original bottom pile at the beginning? No problem. Simply turn all the piles up, using the same actions, but don't do the move. He must lose, because he has a deuce. (Remember, there are no ties; so even if you had a deuce also, you'd still win.)

Then gather the cards, and set another low card beneath the ace during a shuffle, and repeat. He won't select the original bottom pile the second time!

Afterthoughts:—Just a little tip to make it easier to steal just one card. As the packet is being turned, lift *up* slightly with the thumb, *then* apply pressure. Once the face card *clears* the other cards by even an eighth of an inch, you've made sure that only that one card will stay in your hand when the thumb presses it against the palm.

Incidentally, I've found that if you cut the deck so that the vital packet is in the *center*, the move really flows. Turn the first packet, go to the second, doing the move, and then turn the third. Try it, and use the method you like better.

Try this move; it's the sort of thing that makes you feel good when it works well!

After playing with it for a bit, I liked it so much that I wanted another way to use it—maybe with a selected card instead of the gambling presentation. (Not at the same sitting, of course.)

I came up with one quickie that you might like. For the record, call it

TO CHANGE A CARD

Just a quick description:—Control a selected card to the top. You'll have to know what it is, so either force it, or peek it after you've controlled it.

Cut the deck into three piles as explained, except do it *face up* this time. Like this: Let's assume that the selected card is the 5H. Cut the deck, face up, with the right hand. But when you're forming the second pile, riffle the inner left corners upward with the right thumb tip. If you lean back just a bit, you'll be able to see the indices. (See Fig. 164).

The idea is to get another 5-spot to the face of this second pile.

Or—if you can't find a 5-spot (or even if you can), then the 4H or 6H will do. (It might even be better that way—the change is more startling from a 4- or 6-spot to a 5-spot, than from the 5D to the 5H, etc.) The point is, I want a card *as close to his card* as I can find quickly, on the face of this pile. (Be sure that the cards on the first and third piles are not similar to his.)

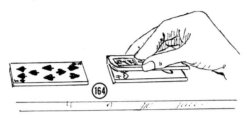

Okay; when you spot a card you want, cut there and place the remaining cards to the right. The situation is:—You've got the selected card at the *rear* of the first pile, and a similar card at the *face* of the second (center) pile.

Now, say to the spectator, "Which of these three cards is closest to the card you're thinking of? Don't tell me the name of your card; just which of these is closest."

Of course, he'll indicate that center pile. Say, "Oh good; that's closest to it; not the 8D, but the 4H, and not the KC—"

As you say this, and as you name the cards (of course, you name the cards that are visible)—turn the piles down, doing the move as explained. This steals the selected card from the rear of the first pile and places it to the face of the center one.

All right; the three piles are now face down. Patter:— "I wanted to change one of those three cards to your card, by magic of course—and it's much easier to do that with a card that *already* looks something like yours! (?) This is the one, right? (Point to the center pile.) All right; watch!"

Ask for the name of his card; snap your fingers, or gesture, over the center pile, then turn it up to show that the similar card has indeed changed to his card!

Well, there you have it. It's interesting to note that with the deck face down, in the gambling presentation, a card is changed by *removing* another card. In my effect, with the deck face up, a card is changed by *adding* another card.

You might like to try to come up with an effect or two yourself, utilizing this move. You might even try stealing a card from the first *and* second piles!

DEAL & DUCK

My good friend, Bill Simon, has graciously given me his permission to include this. He called it "The Four Queens" when he put it in his latest book, *Mathematical Magic* (published by Scribners).

In a letter to me, Bill wrote that the only reason he used Queens in his description instead of aces, is that "the world is too d—n full of four-ace tricks already!" I must agree with him, of course—except that to the layman, for some reason, a trick having to do with four of a kind, is just a tiny bit more impressive when the four of a kind are aces. Anyway, for this effect particularly, I always use the aces.

I haven't changed the basic effect and method at all. I've added the presentation and a touch or two here and there, and it's both a fooler *and* entertaining. I'll explain it just as I do it.

First of all, get the four aces out of the deck and into your lap. See "Oh, Those Aces" for my thoughts on this. Keep in mind that if you're seen stealing the aces, you'll ruin this.

Hand the deck to the spectator, who should be sitting opposite you at the table. Tell him to shuffle thoroughly and then cut the deck into two halves. He's to keep one half and hand you the other.

Your hands go under the table with your half and tell him to do the same. As you go under the table, put the aces on top of your half. Loudly riffle shuffle your cards under the table, leaving the aces on top.

Bring out one ace, face down, and place it on the table near you. Tell your spectator to bring out any one of his cards, just as you did. Reach under, and bring out another ace, telling your spectator to bring out another of his cards.

Repeat this a third time. Now, under the table, spread your cards and place the last ace in the center of the spread, but stepped up a bit so you can spot it. (See Fig. 165). Come out with all the cards, remove the ace and tell your spectator to take one more from his cards.

This is just a touch to prove(?) that you're taking cards from just anywhere. Don't stress this, or say anything. Removing this last card from the center speaks for itself. There is now a face down, four-card packet (aces) in front of you, and a face down, four-card packet (indifferent cards) in front of the spectator.

Push your packet to him and tell him to shuffle each packet separately, "Which is silly, of course, since neither of us knows what those cards are." He now has the two four-card packets in front of him.

Tell him that he's to place either one of the packets onto the other, forming one packet of eight cards. "However, in case you think it would help me to know which packet goes onto which— don't do it until my back is turned." Turn your back while he does this.

Now, keep in mind that you're sitting opposite your spectator. As I explain, when I tell you to point to a spot on the table (between you and him) that is to *your* right, that will mean the spectator's left, and vice versa. I'll keep reminding you of this. Have the spectator hold the packet, face down, in his hands.

Patter:—"In order to be a magician, you've got to be lucky. I'm about to see if you're lucky with cards. This is a test, really. We're going to deal those eight cards, which were selected at random and which you've shuffled, back into two packets of four cards each. I'll tell you just how we'll do it. First, we'll deal two cards here (point to your right; his left), one at a time. Then two here (point to your left; his right), one at a time. Then we'll finish by dealing cards, singly and alternately, onto the two packets, until each one has four cards." (Do *not* point at all during the last sentence.)

"Okay. Not only that, but I'll give you a choice as to which card is dealt, each time. Now I told you we would deal two cards here (point to your right), one at a time. Let's deal the first one, *but*, here's your choice. Would you rather deal the top card down here and then 'duck' the next one to the bottom (of the packet), or—would you rather duck the top card first and then deal the *next* one down? In other words, would you rather deal and then duck, or duck and then deal?"

Let him answer first, then, *whichever* he says, "Deal and duck" or "duck and deal," allow him to do it. Help him this first time, so he knows just what you're talking about. If he decides to deal first, be sure he ducks the next card. (This holds true each time. Whenever he *deals* first, he *must* duck the next card.)

"All right; now we have to deal another card onto that one. Which do you want to do, deal and duck, or duck and deal?" Let him answer first, then let him do whichever he chooses. There are now two face down cards, one on top of the other, to your right, his left.

"Now, as I told you, we'll 'deal two cards, in the same manner, over here." (Point to the left of the first two cards.) "For the first card, do you want to deal and duck, or duck and deal? And incidentally, you realize, don't you, that if I want you to deal and duck and you decide to duck and deal—I'm a dead duck!"

This is said tongue-in-cheek, of course, and *should* get a laugh. Let him tell you which he wants to do—and let him do it. Now give him his choice as to what he wants to do for the second card in that pile. There are now two packets consisting of two cards each, on the table. (See Fig. 166).

"Now, let's deal another card apiece onto each pile. Do you want to deal and duck, or duck and deal?" Let him do as he chooses as you indicate the pile to your right. Remind him, about here, that he's dealing each card according to his *own* decision.

Point to the left packet, and repeat exactly with another card. There are now three cards in each packet.

"Now we have to deal another card apiece onto each pile; right? All right; which would you rather do, deal and duck or duck and deal?" You do *not* point to any packet here.

This is the one and only point in the routine where you must control the dealing of a card. The card on top of the two in his hand *must* go onto the packet to your *right* (his left).

If he answers, "Deal and duck," at this point—simply point to the packet to your right, and say, "All right, go ahead deal the card. Of course the last one goes here." (Point to the packet to your left.)

If he says, "Duck and deal," you nonchalantly point to the packet to your *left*, and say the same thing. Or, you might say, "Okay go ahead and duck the top card; now deal the next one here (pointing to the packet to your left) for a change." Either way, that top card must go onto the packet to your right.

There are other ways to accomplish this if he says, "Duck and deal;" switching the packets, etc.; but the easiest way is as I've just explained.

Just be sure you don't point to any particular packet when you're giving him the choice on this next-to-last card. Wait for his choice, then act accordingly.

This is the reason for always making him state his choice first, before he deals. He becomes accustomed to this, so it doesn't seem strange at this point—when you *must* hear his choice first.

All right; there are two packets of four cards each on the table. And *one of these consists of the four aces!* This has happened *automatically,* if you've followed these instructions.

You have no idea *which* is the four-ace packet, and it doesn't matter! Here's how I end:—

Patter:—"Now, you've had your choice all the way down the line. Let's see how lucky you've been and how lucky you are. Push either of those packets toward me."

Pick up the packet that he pushes to you and start to turn it face up. The moment you see whether the face card is an ace or an indifferent card—you immediately say the appropriate thing.

If it's an indifferent card—"Well, you certainly *are* lucky! These four which you've discarded are all mixed; but look at the four you kept." Let him turn up the packet he 'kept' (or you do it) to expose the four aces. (See Fig. 167).

If you see an ace as you turn the packet he's pushed toward you—"Well, you certainly *are* lucky! Look at the packet you selected; the four aces! Had you selected the other packet, you could never be a magician, because it consists of indifferent cards only."

So you see, it doesn't matter which packet contains the aces or which one he pushes toward you!

Just remember that your remark at the end must come *as* you turn the packet over and it must seem as if that's the way you *always* end it. Once you start turning it over, don't hesitate, start talking and continue turning it until it's face up on the table.

You've got a double-barrelled climax here; first of course is the fact that the four aces are all in one packet after the spectator shuffled and dealt the cards just as he wanted. Second, the fact that the aces are *there* at all! This will take a moment to sink in, after the first climax. *Then* your audience will realize that the spectator shuffled the deck at the start, etc., etc., so how did the aces get there at all!?

Afterthoughts:—You can, if you like, start with the four aces on top instead of lapping them. Do a couple of jog shuffles, let the spectator cut the deck into halves and you take the original top half. It's much stronger, done as I've explained; that is, 'going south' with the aces.

Also—all the "your right" and "your left" business I included in the text is simply to get the situation clear in your mind. Once it is clear—forget it. It doesn't matter at all, you see, whether you start him dealing the packets to the right or left. As long as you follow through once you start. That is; two cards, two cards, one card, one card, and then the last two cards, one to a packet.

The next-to-last card must go onto the *first* packet of two cards he dealt, whether it's to your left or to your right. If you turn the four aces face up and run through the routine once or twice, by yourself, it will become as clear as the sound made by most magicians doing the 'pass.'

At the start, where I told you to put the last ace into the spread so it will appear as if it's coming from anywhere in the deck—this must be done quickly and without looking, of course. That's the way I do it, but if you find it awkward, you can simply put the ace near center and hold a break above it. Then come out and spread up to it. Either way is all right. Just so it appears as if you're removing a card at random.

Finally—you understand, I'm sure, that this works automatically (except for that next-to-last card) no matter *which* choice he makes as to deal and duck or duck and deal. Familiarize yourself with this routine, then try it. I think you'll want to use it often.

LAST WORD

IT CONTINUALLY amazes me when I fool magicians with effects from my books, which they tell me they've read. And I present the effects exactly as I described them in the books.

When I make them aware of this fact—the excuse usually is that they just never *tried* that particular effect and proceeded to forget it. I mention this only for the opportunity to repeat (I've said it in every one of my books) that you must *try* the effects, not just read them.

It's difficult for most magicians to decide whether a particular effect or routine is good for them by just reading it. So learn these and *try* them! If you don't, you may miss out on something that's 'right up your alley.'

Of course, you *must* practice and learn the effects first. Admittedly, some of the effects in this book are not easy to do, or learn. But as I've said before, nothing worthwhile usually *is*. And—these should keep you busy for a while.

The effects I've included here are of my own conception unless otherwise mentioned. Many times of course, an existing idea—something I've seen, heard or read—will trigger my thinking, either consciously or subconsciously. Wherever possible or plausible, I mention the thing, idea or person that triggered the routine I've come up with. I've tried to do this in all my books. If I've neglected to do so anywhere, it was (and is) inadvertent, and I apologize now.

The effects in this book that I, personally, use most often are, Foursome, Favorite Aces & Kings, 1-2-3 Aces, The Indicator, Ten Card Poker Deal and Faro Blockbuster—in about that order.

In my (partial) opinion, these are reputation-making effects, when done well. They've been so for me, anyway.

I've written this book mainly because of the fantastic and gratifying response to my first three magic books. And—because of the many, many requests for me to do another. I sincerely hope that you find this one to be as worthwhile, interesting and stimulating as you seemed to find my other books.

If you do—and let me know it—who knows, I may even write another one!

CLOSE-UP CARD MAGIC
(HARRY LORAYNE)

Straight from the pen of this Master Card Worker comes a new book which we feel sure will become a popular reference source for all that is best in CLOSE-UP CARD MAGIC. If you are interested in Card Magic at all, you MUST have this book. Guaranteed to give you more useful, entertaining, audience preferred card effects, than any other book available. 272 pages full of astounding effects, routines, ideas by Harry Lorayne and some of his friends, including some of the best minds in Card Magic; Dai Vernon, Francis Carlyle, Johnny Benzais, Frank Garcia, Herb Zarrow, Alex Elmsley, Al Leech, Jay Ose, Sam Schwartz, Ken Krenzel, Howard Schwarzman, Bill Simon, Walter Cummings, Paul Curry, Oscar Weigle and others.

Chapter for chapter, page for page, line for line, the most clearly and concisely written and best magic content of ANY book you've ever possessed. Effective card mysteries you will do immediately, unique card tricks with which you will bewilder your friends, novel card mysteries you may have seen the experts do, all these revealed in this beautiful 272 page, easy to understand, DELUXE EDITION.

One of the many unsolicited letters we have received praising "Close-Up Card Magic,"

Gentlemen:

My delight shall not be stifled! Just two days ago I opened a parcel in which was contained "Close-Up Card Magic." In this tiny span of time, I have read virtually the whole volume. My response is one of delight, enthusiasm and shocked surprise. For it is rare indeed when I purchase a card book and find more than one (or two at the most) items really practical and worthwhile. Hence, the "shocked surprise."

Upon opening the volume, I chanced to open it to "Out Of This Universe," and began reading it with only casual interest. (I'm used to being disappointed when reading magical literature.) Suffice it to say it was a bare few lines before this casual interest changed to something bordering on ecstasy or sublimity. Should someone call forth the demons and render the rest of the pages blank, I already knew that I had received far more than my ten bucks worth from this treatise. This little number is one of those rare niceties upon which one chances but once in a million lines.

But the demons were kind and "Vernon's Aces," Elmsley's "No Looking," Lorayne's "Push Through Poker," and countless others were not to be held back. By golly, though I can hardly believe it, here is a book which contains not one, but innumerable beautiful, practical, workable and magical effects with playing cards.

In conclusion, let me say that my thanks is monumental; my joy irrepressible; and my lost love for magical literature revived.

Very truly yours, Berk Davis, Jackson, Mississippi

P. S. I have but one regret: Being a selfish critter, I wish that you had priced this item at, say, $50.00 (more nearly its real value), for then it would have fallen into only the more appreciative hands—but then, as you say, you need the money!

The new Harry Lorayne book—272 pages—135 illustrations by Ed Mishell, edited by Lou Tannen. . . . . DELUXE EDITION $10.00

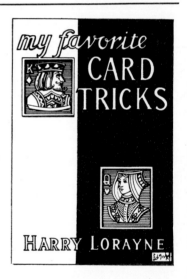

STARS OF MAGIC SERIES

Here's the creme de la creme of the magic world by its leading performers. The absolute ultimate in the impromptu, sleight of hand, no special props category. Beautifully and completely photographed by George Karger, and edited by George Starke. Equal to personal instructions. Over 340 Photos.

No. 1—SCARNE SERIES

1—Classic Ball Routine $3.00
2—Silver and Copper Coin Routine $3.00
3—Triple Coincidence Card Effect $1.00

No. 2—1st DAI VERNON SERIES

1—Triumph Card Miracle $2.00
2—Cutting the Aces ..$2.00
3—Spellbound, Coin Routine $2.00
4—Kangaroo Coins, Coins Thru Table $2.00

No. 3—ALLERTON, HORO-WITZ, JARROW SERIES

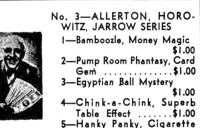

1—Bamboozle, Money Magic $1.00
2—Pump Room Phantasy, Card Gem $1.00
3—Egyptian Ball Mystery $1.00
4—Chink-a-Chink, Superb Table Effect $1.00
5—Hanky Panky, Cigarette Penetration $1.00

No. 4—CARLYLE SERIES

1—Decapitation, Match Wizardry $1.00
2—Homing Card Sensational $1.00
3—Wrist Watch Steal & Coin Routine $2.00

No. 5—2nd Dai Vernon SERIES

1—Cups and Balls Routine, Impromptu $5.00
2—Ambitious Card, Terrific $2.00
3—Mental Card Miracle $3.00

No. 6—3rd DAI VERNON SERIES

1—Ring On Wand, Six Impromptu Methods ..$5.00
2—Slow Motion 4 Aces $4.00
3—The Travellers, Card Feat $3.00

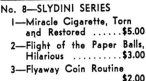

No. 7—DR. DALY SERIES

1—Cards Up The Sleeve $5.00
2—Itinerant Pasteboard $3.00
3—Cavorting Aces $3.00

No. 8—SLYDINI SERIES

1—Miracle Cigarette, Torn and Restored $5.00
2—Flight of the Paper Balls, Hilarious $3.00
3—Flyaway Coin Routine $2.00

No. 9—ROSS BERTRAM ON COINS

Five complete feature coin effects. Rubdown, Doublecross, Passing the Half backs, The Porous Pan, Coin Assembly. 12 pages. Complete ...$8.00

No. 10—VERNON ON MALINI SERIES

3 Miracle Effects, Malini's Own Color Change, Impossible vanish of a coin and Blindfold Card Stabbing Trick. Each with the famous Malini touch. Complete $10.00

No. 11—VERNON ON LEIPZIG SERIES

4 Effects. Leipzig's opener and Leipzig's Acrobat Card Sensation. Stack of coins thru hand and torn and restored cigarette paper. Masterpieces of Magic. Only $10.00

All the above effects are of course sold separately, but now comes the greatest offer in magic. All of them, $94.00 worth are yours for a mere $25.00 if purchased at one time. This is less than 66¢ a trick, complete in binder. Thousands paid the full $94.00, now you can have it for a mere pittance. The Complete Series **$12.50**

It is important for the student of magic to possess a knowledge of the fundamentals of the art—the basic principles of sleight of hand, and the modus operandi of the standard devices and utility pieces of apparatus generally used in producing magical effects.

In the following book list will be found works on every phase of magic, and the kindred arts. A reading of the subjects in which you are particularly interested, will give you valuable instructions and secrets worth many times the mere cost of the book. The greater your knowledge of magic, the better will you be able to select the apparatus for your programs, and thus secure the best results from the amount invested.

HARLAN TARBELL
—Author

RALPH W. READ
—Editor

LOUIS TANNEN
—Publisher

The TARBELL COURSE IN MAGIC

is the

FIRST CHOICE

among books on

The Art of Magic, Sleight of Hand, Pocket, Parlor and Stage Tricks, Illusions, etc.

Dr. Harlan Tarbell, author, Ralph W. Read, editor, and Louis Tannen, publisher of these great works, have combined to give you . . . .

ALL THE SECRETS OF THE MAGIC ART

SEE FOLLOWING PAGE FOR FULL DETAILS - - - - - - -

• MAGIC BOOKS •

Volume 1 — 19 Lessons — 410 Pages — 918 Illustrations — $7.50

1. History of Magic
2. Magic as a Science
3. Sleight of Hand with Coins
4. Coin Tricks
5. More Coin Tricks
6. The Thumb Tip
7. Impromptu Tricks
8. Ball Tricks
9. Mathematical Mysteries
10. Effective Card Mysteries
11. Impromptu Card Mysteries
12. Mental Card Mysteries
13. Card Sleights
14. Novel Card Mysteries
15. Restoring Torn Papers
16. Rope & Tape Principle
17. Handkerchief Tricks
18. Knotty Silks
19. Eggs and Silks

Volume 2 — 14 Lessons — 410 Pages — 1087 Illustrations — $10.00

20. How to Please Your Audience
21. Magic with Wands
22. Double Paper Mysteries—many deceptive effects
23. Magic with Coins
24. Cigarette Magic, with lighted and unlighted cigarettes
25. Sleight of Hand with Cards— back palm, seconds, etc.
26. Selected Card Mysteries
27. Rising Cards (17 methods)
28. Egg Magic—Tarbell's Egg Bag —Unbreakable Egg, etc.
29. Billiard Ball Manipulation
30. Handkerchief Magic, De Luxe
31. Rope Magic—new, clever
32. "Ghostlite" Mysteries
33. Illusions—low cost effects

Volume 3 — 12 Lessons — 418 Pages — 1116 Illustrations — $10.00

34. Routining a Magic Show
35. How to Make People Laugh
36. Intimate Magic
37. Conjuring with Currency
38. Modern Coin Effects
39. Fundamental Card Sleights
40. Card Mysteries
41. Card Stabbing
42. Novelty Handkerchief Magic
43. Color Changing Silks
44. Rabbit and Dove Magic
45. Illusions

Volume 4 — 13 Lessons — 418 Pages — 1140 Illustrations — $10.00

46. Novelty Magic, wide variety
47. Thimble Magic—complete act
48. Swallowing Needles & Blades
49. Unique Card Magic
50. Novelty Rising Cards
51. Card Transition Tricks
52. Mental & Psychic Mysteries
53. The Thumb Tie—10 Methods
54. Chinese Linking Rings
55. Magic With Ribbon
56. Silken Trickery, De Luxe
57. Slate Tricks, new & novel Methods with 1 & 2 slates, etc.
58. Illusions—Fu Manchu's

Volume 5 — 13 Lessons — 418 Pages — 1152 Illustrations — $10.00

59. Unique Magic
60. More Unique Mysteries
61. Four-Ace Effects
62. Modern Mental Mysteries
63. Hat and Coat Productions
64. Oriental Magic
65. Original Oriental Secrets
66. Tarbell Hindu Rope Mysteries
67. Modern Rope Magic
68. Magic of the Bambergs
69. Magic with Bowls and Liquids
70. Illusions
71. Publicity and Promotion

Volume 6 — 10 Lessons — 410 Pages — 1200 Illustrations — $10.00
Edited by BRUCE ELLIOTT

72. Novel Ball Magic
73. Unique Card Effects
74. Novelty Magic
75. Rope Magic
76. Mindreading Mysteries
77. X-Ray Eyes and Blindfold Effects
78. Silk and Rope Penetrations
79. Escapes and Substitutions
80. Spirit Ties and Vest Turning
81. Modern Stage Magic
82. Stage Productions
83. Magic as Theatre

Order the entire set and have a complete Encyclopedia of Magic.

The Set **$55.00**

• MAGIC BOOKS •

No. 1463B—ROUTINED MANIPULATION PART ONE (Ganson)

This wonderful book of photo illustrated magic is completely routined and well deserves the popularity that has sold out many editions. A great cigarette routine, terrific routine with the multiplying candles, card manipulation, Miser's dream and many others with photos showing each and every move. Highly recommended. 118 pages, 167 illustrations.

A low **$2.50**

No. 1464B—ROUTINED MANIPULATION PART TWO (Ganson)

If you have part one you'll demand part two. The tops in manipulative magic. Ask the boys who have it. This volume contains effects with balls, thimbles, handkerchiefs, knives, ropes, cards and all completely explained, routined with every move, sleight, and action photographed. Egg bag routine is unique, and the sections on Billiard Balls and thimbles as well as the card section are simply out of this world. 133 pages, illus. . . . . Price **$3.00**

No. 1465B—ROUTINED MANIPULATION "FINALE" (Ganson)

The tremendous success of the two "ROUTINED MANIPULATION" books resulted in requests from all over the world for "another one, please!" Well, Lewis has obliged! AND WHAT A BOOK!

He presents an enormous amount of magnificent material and photographs, to make up the BIGGEST and BEST of the wonderful "Routined Manipulation" series.

A galaxy of Star Magicians gave their best material . . . Fred Kaps . . . Jack Chanim . . . Gerald Kosky . . . Al Koran . . . Ken Brooks . . . Peter and Elizabeth Warlock . . . Alexander Elmsley . . . Peter Burto . . . Hans Trixer . . . Billy McComb . . . Douglas Francis . . . etc., tec.

Included also, is LEWIS GANSON'S own method for the PRODUCTION OF CARDS . . . brilliant material and Photographs. Six Chapters giving every detail necessary for performing this spectacular Card Act.

The text has been so written that every move is very easy to understand, whilst the Photographs ensure that every detail is crystal clear. This book TEACHES HOW TO PERFORM the wonderful Routines . . . almost equal to personal instruction.

Lewis Ganson has surpassed himself with "FINALE" . . . he presents a book of magic that will earn for itself the proud title of a "Classic of Magic" . . . a book that will be cherished by the discerning magician for the years to come . . . priceless material that will be USED. A book that will be talked of with pride wherever and whenever magicians meet.

- • 256 Pages . . .
  - • Over 250 Photogrphic Illustrations . . .
    - • Full Page Photographs of Famous Magic Contributors.

One of the finest examples of Magic Book Craftsmanship ever published. Price **$6.00**